Sedley Taylor, Archibald Briggs

Profit-sharing between capital and labour

Six essays

Sedley Taylor, Archibald Briggs
Profit-sharing between capital and labour
Six essays

ISBN/EAN: 9783337229504

Printed in Europe, USA, Canada, Australia, Japan

Cover: Foto ©Suzi / pixelio.de

More available books at **www.hansebooks.com**

PROFIT-SHARING

BETWEEN

CAPITAL AND LABOUR,

SIX ESSAYS

BY

SEDLEY TAYLOR, M.A.
LATE FELLOW OF TRINITY COLLEGE, CAMBRIDGE,

TO WHICH IS ADDED A

MEMORANDUM
ON
THE INDUSTRIAL PARTNERSHIP AT THE
WHITWOOD COLLIERIES
(1865–1874)
BY
ARCHIBALD BRIGGS AND THE LATE HENRY CURRER BRIGGS,

TOGETHER WITH

REMARKS ON THE MEMORANDUM
BY
SEDLEY TAYLOR.

LONDON
KEGAN PAUL, TRENCH & CO., 1, PATERNOSTER SQUARE
1884

TO MY FRIEND

THE RIGHT HONOURABLE

HENRY FAWCETT, M.P.,

PROFESSOR OF POLITICAL ECONOMY IN THE UNIVERSITY
OF CAMBRIDGE,

ONE OF THE EARLIEST AND STAUNCHEST SUPPORTERS

OF PROFIT-SHARING,

I DEDICATE THIS VOLUME.

PREFACE.

By directly interesting workmen in the profits which their labour contributes to produce, a group of Continental, and especially of Parisian, firms have introduced a singularly efficacious means of obtaining enhanced industrial results, and of stilling the disastrous antagonism between employers and employed. The particular mode of remunerating labour which has brought these benefits in its train was first put into action by the house-painter Leclaire, in 1842, and is now working in a great variety of productive undertakings, and in one distributive establishment of colossal size. A French Society formed to promote the study of this system has, since 1879, published a quarterly serial describing its progress: its principle and practice have also been investigated by two public commissions appointed by the Prefect of the Seine and the Minister of the Interior, respectively, and by a committee of the Chamber of Deputies.

The Essays contained in the present volume aim at placing before British employers and employed some account of the above movement. The first, second and fifth of them originally appeared in the *Nineteenth Century* and are reprinted by the kind permission of Mr. Knowles. In respect to the third Essay I am indebted for a like concession to the Council of the Manchester Statistical Society. During the process of revision I have corrected a few inaccuracies, struck out repetitions incident to separate publication and brought my facts and figures, as far as possible, to date. The materials for doing this have been mainly obtained by private correspondence with the heads of Continental firms, whose courteous and willing aid I gratefully acknowledge.

I desire to draw special attention to the Memorandum by Messrs. Briggs on the history of the Industrial Partnership which existed at their Collieries, at Whitwood near Normanton, Yorkshire, from 1865 to 1874. The writings of several distinguished Political Economists had given to the early successes of that experiment an European celebrity, and its abandonment necessarily inflicted on participating enterprise a discouragement proportionately severe. Nine years have since elapsed without bringing to the considerable public interested in the subject an authentic account of the causes which led to that memorable breakdown. Such an account is here for the first time published in the most authoritative form, as being the work of the two gentlemen who had continuous charge of the experiment from its inception to its close. The reader, after perusing this Memorandum and the remarks which I have appended to it, will, I am confident, see reason for holding, with Messrs. Briggs, that the reverse sustained at Whitwood affords no rational ground for discouragement as to the future of the participating principle.

If I am right in believing that a wide application of that principle offers a prospect of strengthening, vivifying and purifying productive enterprise to an extent of which we have as yet but a faint conception, the attention of British employers and employed—and indeed of the British public also, in their capacity of consumers,—can hardly be too importunately called to this remedy for industrial evils at a time when we constantly hear of strikes and rumours of strikes, when capital is bitterly denounced on the one side, and the inadequacy and apathy of labour alleged on the other as the cause of a dangerous and growing debility in British manufacture, whether on a great or on a small scale. As a wise organisation of the participating principle is almost as important as the adoption of the principle itself, I have, for the information of those who may be disposed to give it a trial, translated *in extenso* and placed in an Appendix three typical sets of regulations under which it is actually working in as many establishments of the first rank at Paris.

I wish here to express my profound conviction that the methods described in this volume, valuable as they are in themselves, constitute no self-acting panacea; and that their best fruits can be reaped only by men who feel that life does not consist in abundance of material possessions, who regard stewardship as nobler than ownership, who see in the ultimate outcome of all true work issues reaching beyond the limits of the present dispensation, and who act faithfully and strenuously on these beliefs.

TRINITY COLLEGE, CAMBRIDGE,
December, 1883.

CONTENTS.

ESSAY I.
PROFIT-SHARING IN THE MAISON LECLAIRE.

Introduction, pp. 1–3. Life of Leclaire, 3–12. The House and Mutual Aid Society, 13–17. The *noyau, comité de conciliation* and *conseil de famille*, 17–19. Educational and moral results of profit-sharing, 20–23. Economic basis of the system, 23, 24. Leclaire's ultimate aim, 24, 25.

ESSAY II.
PROFIT-SHARING IN INDUSTRY.

Introduction, pp. 26–28. Sources of information, 28, 29. Classification of systems, 29. *Maison Bord*, 30, 31. *Compagnie d'Assurances Générales*, 31–33. *Maison Billon et Isaac*, 33–39. Summary of applications of the system, 39. Its benefits, 40. Fund on which it draws, 41. Conditions favourable to its introduction, and branches of production fulfilling those conditions, 42, 43.

ESSAY III.
PROFIT-SHARING IN INDUSTRY—(*Continued*).

Public attention already called to the subject in France, p. 44. *Société de la Participation aux Bénéfices*, 45, 46. Prefect of the Seine's Commission, 47. Chamber of Deputies' Committee, 47–49. Minister of the Interior's *Enquête*, 49, note. *Maison Chaix*, 50–60. Theory and benefits of profit-sharing, 61–66. Objections to the system stated and answered, 66–70. Probable attitude of English Trades Unions, 71–73. Opinions of Professors Jevons and Fawcett, 74, 75.

ESSAY IV.

PROFIT-SHARING IN THE PARIS AND ORLEANS RAILWAY COMPANY.

First introduction of the principle in 1844, and division of *employés* into three classes for profit-sharing purposes, pp. 77, 78. Alteration of system in 1847, 79. Abandonment of division into classes in 1848, 79. Regulations of 1850, 1853 and 1854, 80, 81. Fundamental change of system in 1863, 81, 82. Material results of profit-sharing, 82, 83. Influence of the regulation of 1863, 83, 84. Historical summary, and present condition, of participation in the Company, 84-86.

ESSAY V.

PROFIT-SHARING IN AGRICULTURE.

Promising field offered by agriculture, pp. 87, 88. Herr von Thünen's farm, 88-91. Herr Jahnke's farm, 91-94. Opinion of Herr Wölbling, 94, 95. Baron Zytphen-Adeler's farm, 95-97. May success in participatory agriculture be looked for in this country? 98, 99.

APPENDIX TO ESSAY V.

Mr. Vandeleur's Irish experiment, 100-108.

ESSAY VI.

PROFIT-SHARING IN DISTRIBUTIVE ENTERPRISE.

The *Maison Boucicaut*, or *Magasin du Bon Marché*, p. 110. Life of its founder, 110, 111. The Provident Society, its objects and organisation, 112, 113. Conditions and extent of participation, 114. Material results attained, 115. Further development introduced since the death of M. Boucicaut, 115. Applicability of profit-sharing to co-operative stores, 116.

MESSRS. BRIGGS' MEMORANDUM ON INDUSTRIAL PARTNERSHIP AT THE WHITWOOD COLLIERIES.

Introduction, p. 117. Terms of profit-sharing announced in prospectus of 1864, 118: material results from 1865 to 1872, 119, 120. Inflation in the coal trade: rise of wages and increase made in rate of initial interest on capital: material results of 1873 and 1874, 120, 121. Decline of prices, Strike against reduction of wages and abandonment of profit-sharing, 121, 122. Causes which led to this result:—First collision with the Miners' Union, 123, 124. The 'riddles' dispute;

CONTENTS. xiii

intervention by the Union leaders, 126–128. Strike against the Company and suppression of profit-sharing, 129. Conclusion, 130, 131. Explanatory note by Mr. Archibald Briggs, 131, 132.

REMARKS ON MESSRS. BRIGGS' MEMORANDUM.

Great celebrity of the Whitwood experiment, p. 133. Conditions under which it originated, 135, 136. Material and moral results during first three years, 136–138. Supplementary statement by Mr. Archibald Briggs, 139. Circumstances which probably contributed to the final breakdown:—Increase made in rate of initial interest on capital, 141–144. Coincidence of dates fixed for Shareholders' and Miners' Union meetings, 145–147. The 'riddles' dispute, 147, 148. Conflict with the Miners' Union, 148–151. Criticism on the foregoing remarks by Mr. Archibald Briggs, 152–154.

APPENDIX OF REGULATIONS.

PAGES

No. 1. MAISON A. BORD. (Immediate Participation.) ... 157, 158
No. 2. COMPAGNIE D'ASSURANCES GÉNÉRALES. (Deferred Participation.) 159–163
No. 3. MAISON A. CHAIX ET COMPAGNIE. (Mixed Participation.) 164–170

PROFIT-SHARING.

ESSAY I.

PROFIT-SHARING IN THE MAISON LECLAIRE.

(*Nineteenth Century*, September, 1880.)

THE principle of participation by workmen in the profits of their employers, which was first tentatively put into operation by the Parisian house-decorator Leclaire in 1842, has since that time made signal progress. According to recent information, upwards of fifty industrial establishments in France, Alsace and Switzerland alone are now working upon this principle. The material advantages accruing both to employers and employed from systems of participation have been distinctly recognised by English writers on political economy—Babbage, Mill, Fawcett and others—but the intellectual and moral benefits which attach to the best existing methods of applying the principle have not, in this country at least, as yet attracted a degree of public attention at all commensurate with their importance. A lecture* addressed to an audience of working men in Cambridge on the 9th of December, 1879, by Mr. W. H. Hall, contains, in a biographical form, an excellent sketch of the development of Leclaire's institution, and faithfully reflects the spirit which animates it. From this lecture I received a strong impulse to make a personal examination, on the actual scene of Leclaire's labours, into the most recent results there attained. On making my wish known through Mr. Hall to the present heads of Leclaire's house, I received from them a most cordial invitation, coupled with an offer to place their time and information unreservedly at my disposal. When, in the spring of 1880, I presented myself to these gentlemen at Paris, they proved in every respect as good as their word. I was allowed free access to the accounts of the establishment and to every source of information for which I chose to ask; my long string of questions, too, were answered with thorough-going fulness and unwearied patience. It is entirely owing to the kindness of MM. Redouly et Marquot, managing partners of the house of Leclaire, and of M. Charles Robert, President of the Mutual Aid Society connected with it, that I am enabled to make known, in the most authentic shape, the present condition of perhaps the most beneficent industrial foundation now extant. To M. Marquot, who received me in the absence of his senior colleague, and to M. Charles Robert, my heartiest

* Published as a pamphlet by the Central Co-operative Board, Manchester.

thanks are due for considerate attention and unfailing courtesy.

As a condition of understanding the present working of Leclaire's institution, some preliminary study must be devoted to the facts of its historical development. These, again, are inextricably interwoven with the incidents of Leclaire's life. I have accordingly found it indispensable, before describing his establishment as it actually exists, to narrate those facts of his life which bear most directly on the development of participation. In doing this I have, with the author's express permission, made full, and in places direct translational, use of the excellent French biography of Leclaire * written by his ardent admirer and disciple, M. Charles Robert. English readers will find interesting details, which I am obliged to pass over here, in Mr. Hall's lecture already referred to.†

Edme-Jean Leclaire was born on the 14th of May, 1801. The son of a poor village shoemaker, he was removed from school at ten years old, with the scantiest knowledge even of reading and writing, and put to work, first in the fields and next as a mason's apprentice. At seventeen, having arrived penniless and unfriended at Paris, he apprenticed himself to a house-painter. After three years passed amidst much privation under a hard master, Leclaire became a journeyman, and after seven more, when only twenty-six years of age, took the bold step of setting up in

* *Leclaire, Biographie d'un Homme Utile.* Paris, Sandoz et Fischbacher, 1878.

† They may also consult a more recent pamphlet by Miss Mary H. Hart, *A Brief Sketch of the Maison Leclaire* (London, 405, Oxford Street, 1882).

business on his own account. Extraordinary capacity, energy and daring enabled him to force his way with signal success and celerity. Within three years' time he had attracted the notice of architects by the excellence of the work done under his direction, and was already employed on considerable undertakings. In 1834 he was called on to execute works at the Bank of France and on the buildings of several railway companies: in fact by this time his success as an employer of labour was definitively assured.

Even had Leclaire done nothing more than this, he would have deserved a high place among the heroes of "self-help," who, though destitute of all extraneous aid, have by innate force and indomitable perseverance fought their way from penury to posts of industrial command. But Leclaire was far indeed from contenting himself with the part of a mere *exploiteur* of other men's labour. No sooner was his own position as an industrial chief assured, than, with rare width and generosity of view, he threw himself into plans and efforts for raising the condition of his own workmen, and ultimately of the wage-earning class in general. I have said that the scope of this Essay permits me to dwell only on those steps taken by Leclaire which directly forwarded the principle of participation; it is, however, impossible to pass over without incidental notice an innovation of his in a different field which has permanently benefited a whole group of workers—the substitution, in the painting trade, of white of zinc for white of lead. Leclaire, having convinced himself that as long as an active poison formed an ingredient in the paints employed, the ravages which it inflicted on workmen could only be palliated, never effectually counteracted, resolved to make search for some innocuous substitute for white of lead. Though totally ignorant of chemistry, he succeeded, with the help of experts whom he called to his aid, in discovering how to utilise white of zinc for this purpose, *i.e.* how to procure it sufficiently cheap, and make it dry with sufficient rapidity. Armed with these results he entirely suppressed the use of white of lead in his establishment, and thereby, as far as his own workmen were concerned, put a stop for the future to 'painter's colic' and all its train of attendant and consequent miseries. I am assured by M. Marquot not only that the white of zinc now exclusively used by the house is perfectly innocuous to the health of the painters, but that work executed with it is both fresher and more durable than that done with the old deleterious ingredient.

Decisively efficacious as was the sympathy which Leclaire felt for the physical sufferings of his workmen, it was the precariousness of the tenure under which they gained their livelihood that caused him the most poignant solicitude. His attention was early fixed on the calamitous effect which the sale of a business has upon the old hands who have been employed under it, when the new master dismisses without mercy every workman whose appearance indicates a diminishing capacity for labour. "A dismissal of this kind," wrote Leclaire in 1865, "inflicts a terrible blow on the workman who undergoes it. From this fatal day he acquires the sad conviction that, go where he may to ask for work, the conclusion will be instantly drawn from his face and bearing that he is too old to do the work well."

Knowing that a workman with children or infirm relatives to maintain could not make the least saving for the time of old age, and perfectly aware of the fate which, on his own retirement, would overtake many of those whose labour had contributed to place him in a position to pass his old days happily, Leclaire centred his attention on schemes for supplying the more providently disposed among his workmen with the means of an assured future. The first impulse in the direction which his plan ultimately took came from a M. Frégier, who, in 1835, told Leclaire that he saw no way to get rid of the antagonism which existed between workman and master except *the participation of the workman in the profits of the master*. From this time forward Leclaire was constantly "cudgelling his brains" (*se frapper le front*) to find the best means of bringing this idea into practical operation.

In 1842 he prepared the ground for his first experiment by a very remarkable proceeding. Frauds were at that time numerous in the painting trade, and Leclaire foresaw that his scheme of participation would be set down as an attempt to enlist the cupidity of workmen by the prospect of illicit gain. Accordingly he proceeded to publish several pamphlets, exposing in the most unreserved manner the secrets of dozens of ways in which high pay could be got for bad work, even on orders secured by enormous reductions in price. By these publications Leclaire, to use his own words, "compelled people to be honest," and made it next to impossible for his workmen to swerve from the rule which he constantly impressed upon them —that the most complete honesty should characterise all their relations with the customers of the house.

On the 15th of February, 1842, Leclaire announced his intention of dividing among a certain number of his *ouvriers* and *employés* a part of the profits produced by the work done. The police, who saw in this nothing but a craftily constructed scheme for enticing workmen away from other masters, did their best to thwart Leclaire's presumed designs by prohibiting a meeting of his *employés* which he had asked permission to hold for the purpose of explaining the advantages attaching to his plan of participation. The meeting was of course abandoned, but Leclaire gave notice that the division of profits on the results of the year 1841 would take place in accordance with his previous announcement. A section of his workmen had from the first distrusted his offers, and they were supported in that attitude by a newspaper, *L'Atelier*, which accused him of manœuvring in this fashion in order to reduce wages. When however Leclaire, after collecting his participants, forty-four in number, threw upon the table a bag of gold containing 11,886 francs (£475), and then and there distributed to each his share, averaging over £10 per man, it was found impossible to withstand the 'object-lesson' thus given. All hesitation vanished and was replaced by unbounded confidence. On the profits of the succeeding years larger sums were divided among increasing numbers of participants. Thus, during the six years from 1842 to 1847 inclusive, an average of £750 was annually divided among an average of eighty persons. The share assigned to each participant was proportional to the sum which he had earned in the shape of wages during the year for which the assessment was made. There were, accordingly, wide differences in the amounts of the bonuses severally received, but the average, for the period above named, came to a little over £9 a year per head.

In 1838 Leclaire had established a 'Mutual Aid Society' for the workmen and *employés* of his house, which was supported by monthly subscriptions from its members, and offered the advantages of an ordinary benefit club. Its statutes provided that a division of the funds of the Society might be demanded at the end of fifteen years from the date of its establishment. Accordingly a liquidation took place in 1853, and the Society was in the following year reconstituted on an entirely new basis. Subscriptions from the members ceased, and the resources of the Society were thenceforth to consist in a share of profits to be freely given by the house at its annual stock-taking.

In 1860 Leclaire, bent on realising his idea of a provision for workmen in their old age, proposed to the members of the Mutual Aid Society that they should relinquish their right to a future division of its funds, and consent to the establishment of retiring pensions. He now found himself in presence of a determined opposition. A capital of about £1600 had accumulated since 1854, and the persons interested in a division declined to forego the considerable sums which it would bring them. The issue was exceedingly critical, for, had the funds of the Society been again dissipated, the most characteristic feature of Leclaire's scheme could hardly have been developed. He had committed a most serious oversight in allowing the right to a subsequent division of funds to remain on the statutes of the Society after its reconstitution in 1854, and he seemed now on the point of being worsted in the decisive battle of his campaign. Fortunately, for the best interests of his opponents even more than for his own, he had reserved to himself the means of victory. He pointed out that though the members of the Society undoubtedly possessed the right of compelling a division of its funds, the statutes had conferred on himself an unlimited power of introducing new members who would be entitled to full shares in the division. By threatening to make a swamping use of this constitutional weapon, and also to withhold the annual subvention hitherto paid by the house, Leclaire induced the recalcitrant members of the Society to give way and consent to the creation of a permanent association and the establishment of retiring pensions.

The next step was to confer on the Society thus reorganised an independent legal status, and, at the same time, to link its interests indissolubly with those of the house from which it sprang. It was registered as an incorporated Society and made a perpetual sleeping partner (*commanditaire*) in the firm of "Leclaire et Compagnie." The words of the founder on handing over the new statutes to the members in 1864 are well worthy of citation here:—

> The members of the Mutual Aid Society are no longer mere journeymen who act like machines and quit their work before

the clock has sounded its last stroke. All have become partners working on their own account: in virtue of this nothing in the workshop ought to be indifferent to them—all should attend to the preservation of the tools and materials as if they were the special keepers of them. . . . If you wish that I should leave this world with a contented heart, it is necessary that you should have realised the dream of my whole life; it is necessary that, after regular conduct and assiduous labour, a workman and his wife should have the wherewithal to live in peace without being a burden upon any one.*

In 1865 Leclaire, who had already devolved the greater part of his duties on the colleague designated as his successor, M. Defournaux, retired to the village of Herblay near Paris, with the avowed intention of accustoming his young institution to walk alone. The following year saw him take a further step in the same direction by resigning his post as President of the Mutual Aid Society in favour of M. Charles Robert, who has occupied it ever since with conspicuous energy and devotion. Leclaire's retirement into country life led however to no cessation, but only to a change, of activity. He was at once appointed *Maire* of Herblay, and spent the two years and a half during which he held office in untiring efforts for the benefit of those placed under his administration.

* "Les membres de la Société de secours mutuels ne sont plus de simples journaliers qui agissent machinalement et qui quittent l'ouvrage avant que l'horloge ait frappé son dernier coup de marteau. Tous sont devenus des associés qui travaillent pour leur propre compte; à ce titre rien dans l'atelier ne doit leur être indifférent : tous doivent veiller au soin des outils et des marchandises comme s'ils en étaient spécialement les gardiens. . . . Si vous voulez que je parte de ce monde le cœur content, il faut que vous ayez réalisé le rêve de toute ma vie; il faut qu'après une conduite régulière et un travail assidu un ouvrier et sa femme puissent, dans leur vieillesse, avoir de quoi vivre tranquilles sans être à charge à personne."

Most of his projects of village reform were successfully carried into effect, but that to which he attached cardinal importance, the application to agriculture of a system of industrial partnership, was not destined to pass, in his hands, beyond the form of an elaborate paper scheme in which he unavailingly urged it on the inhabitants of Herblay.

We have seen that, in 1864, Leclaire gave a permanent legal status to the Mutual Aid Society connected with his house. In 1869 he impressed a like character of perpetuity on the organisation of the house itself. A formal deed enacted that thenceforth the net profits of the business should be divided, in certain fixed proportions, between the managing partners, the Mutual Aid Society and the workmen forming the regular staff of the house. This decisive act of incorporation was preceded by an elaborate inquiry in which every member of the establishment was invited to take part. A printed list of questions on the principal issues involved in the approaching settlement was addressed to each workman, and the answers to these questions, of which about two hundred sets were sent in, were carefully analysed and reported on by a committee appointed for that purpose. The final scheme proposed by Leclaire, which was based on the recommendations of this committee, received the approval of the workmen assembled in a general meeting, and, on the 6th of January, 1869, became the legally binding charter of the house.

Leclaire lived to see his institution pass unscathed through the ordeals of the siege of Paris and the revolutionary conflict of the Commune. During the former calamity, though no longer *Maire* of Herblay, he remained at the village in order to support the inhabitants under the rigours of the German occupation. On the outbreak of the latter he boldly re-entered the capital, determined, "if Paris was to be destroyed, to be buried under its ruins with his workmen."

In the summer of 1872 the heroic old man's health rapidly gave way, and symptoms of the disease which was soon to carry him off began to show themselves. He was able, however, to be present at the annual meeting of his house on the 23rd of June of that year, and to learn that, as the result of the recent stock-taking, £1350 would be paid over to the Mutual Aid Society, and £2700 divided in bonuses to labour. A week before his death, when disease was about to lay its paralysing finger on his restless brain, Leclaire experienced his last earthly happiness in hearing that on the previous day £2000 had been actually distributed among upwards of six hundred workmen, and that there was good reason to believe that the sums so allotted would be either carefully laid by, or applied to the wisest immediate purposes in the homes of the recipients.

Leclaire died at Herblay on the 10th of July, 1872, of apoplexy, in his seventy-second year, and was buried at Paris in the cemetery of Montmartre amidst the tears and outspoken grief of those to whom his life's best energies had been devoted.

In describing the present state of Leclaire's institution, I shall have to dwell with special emphasis on the moral achievements brought about by the administrative machinery with which he supplied it. But before passing from the founder's life to its results, I may with advantage state what, from a purely economic point of view, is sufficiently striking, that during the period from 1842, when he first established participation, until his death in 1872, he had paid over to the Mutual Aid Society, and to his workmen directly, sums amounting in all to not less than £44,000. This was done, too, without impoverishing himself, for he left behind him a private fortune of £48,000.

Leclaire's foundation consists, as has been already seen, of two institutions, closely connected indeed, but separately administered, and capable of independent action—the house, or business-undertaking proper, and the Mutual Aid Society. The capital of the house amounts to £16,000, one-half of which is the property of the two managing partners, MM. Redouly et Marquot, while the other half is held by the Society as sleeping partner. There is also a reserve-fund of £4000, which can be drawn upon in case of an emergency. The Society possessed, in September, 1883, the sum of £62,076, of which about one-third is placed in securities guaranteed by the State, and about two-thirds invested in, or lent upon interest to, the house. The number of members of the Society was at that time 105, not including fifty-one pensioners who were receiving an aggregate of £2060 per annum.

The annual profits made by the house are distributed as follows:—The two managing partners receive £240 each as salaries for superintendence. Interest at five per cent. is paid to them and to the Society on their respective capitals. Of the remaining net profit one quarter goes to MM. Redouly et Marquot jointly, and another quarter to the funds of the Society; the remaining half is divided among all the workmen and others employed by the house, in sums proportionate to the amounts which they have respectively earned in wages, paid at the ordinary market rate, during the year for which the division is being made.

It is important to notice that participation in profits in proportion to wages earned is the right, not only of the corps of picked workmen who form the regular staff of the house, but also of the apprentices, and even of every casual auxiliary picked up, perhaps only for a single day's work, at the street corner. M. Marquot pointed out to me in the books of the house instances of this minute application of the principle, *e.g.* one where a man who had done but *ten hours'* work in 1877 received at the end of that year 1 franc 15 centimes as profits, on 6 francs 50 centimes earned as wages.

Down to 1871 the benefits of participation were restricted to the workmen who formed the permanent staff of the house, but in that year they were thrown open to every man in its employ. The impulse which led to the introduction of this generous measure came, M. Marquot informed me, from a quarter to which Leclaire was ordinarily little disposed to look for inspiration. A socialistic workman not belonging to his establishment had tauntingly said to him in 1870, "Your house is nothing but a box of little masters who make money out of the others." * Leclaire felt the force of this criticism, and determined to make

* "*Votre maison n'est qu'une boîte de petits patrons qui exploitent les autres.*"

employment by the house and participation in profits rigorously coextensive expressions.

The following table shows the sums paid in wages and in bonuses to labour in each year from 1870 to 1882, and the ratios of the latter to the former. The sums are given in English money, true to the nearest pound, and the ratios true to the nearest integer :—

Year.	Number of Participants.	Total of Wages.	Total of Bonuses to Labour.	Ratio of Bonus to Annual Wages.
		£	£	
1870	758	16,257	2331	14 per cent.
1871	1038	22,260	2700	13 ,,
1872	976	29,083	3530	12 ,,
1873	633	20,327	2580	13 ,,
1874	827	24,012	3160	13 ,,
1875	1052	27,862	4000	14 ,,
1876	1081	27,943	4500	16 ,,
1877	826	25,820	4600	18 ,,
1878	1032	28,546	5200	18 ,,
1879	1125	34,715	6400	18 ,,
1880	949	38,897	7600	19 ,,
1881	1125	42,744	8600	20 ,,
1882	998	42,799	9630	22 ,,

The entire sum paid out of profits from the commencement of participation in 1842 down to 1882 inclusive, whether in cash bonuses or to the Mutual Aid Society, was £133,045. The yearly business turn-over of the house, which in the year of Leclaire's death (1872) fell slightly short of £80,000, was in 1882, £125,580.

The Mutual Aid Society confers further conspicuous advantages. Besides performing the functions of an ordinary benefit club, it bestows a retiring life-pension of £48 per annum on every member who has attained the age of fifty and has worked twenty years for the house, and it continues the payment of half this annuity to the widow of such pensioner during her life. It further insures the life of every member for a sum of £40, to be handed over to his family at his death.*

A feature of extraordinary generosity which distinguishes this Society is the following provision. If a workman, even though he be neither member of the Society nor even on the list of those permanently employed by the house, meets while actually engaged in its service with a disabling accident, he becomes at once entitled to the full retiring life-pension of £48, and, if the accident results in his death, a half-pension reverts to his widow. At the annual meeting of the Society on the 4th of April, 1880, I witnessed a striking application of this generous statute. A poor fellow casually called in for an odd job, who never did a stroke of work for the house before, had met with an accident which within a few days put an end to his life. The facts of the case, including a medical certificate as to the cause of death, having been briefly put before the meeting by the President of the Society, the assembled members, by a unanimous show of hands, at once voted to the widow for her life a half-pension of £20.

It results from the preceding statements that a workman in Leclaire's house finds within his reach the following economic benefits, none of which he can look for in an establishment organised on the ordinary system :—

* These pensions stood in 1880 at £40 each; they were raised to £48 on the 1st of January, 1882.

1. A large yearly bonus on his aggregate wages.

2. All the advantages of an ordinary benefit club.

3. A life-pension of £48 from his fiftieth year of age and twentieth year of work, half of which is continued to his widow for her life.

4. £40 payable to his family at his death.

5. The certainty that, if disabled from work by accident encountered when on duty, he will be placed beyond the reach of want, and that, if he be killed, his family will not be left without some permanent means of support.

Conspicuous as are these material advantages, they are far from constituting the whole, or even the principal, good attaching to membership in Leclaire's beneficent institution. Its founder recognised in the principle of participation not merely a means of improving the pecuniary situation of the wage-earning class, but also a powerful lever for raising their moral condition, and with it of course their whole social status. Accordingly he sought to bring that principle into operation in such a form as to constitute an intellectual, moral and almost religious training for all who came into contact with it. A few of the main provisions by which this result has been attained with signal success shall here be briefly described.

Those among the whole number of men employed by the house who prove themselves to be first-rate workmen and of unexceptionable moral conduct can claim admittance into what is called the *noyau*—the kernel or core—of the establishment. The members of the *noyau*, who at present number 126 men, possess

an influential voice in the administration of the house. They form the constituency by whom the *comité de conciliation*, which is for most purposes the governing body of the house, is annually elected. The two managing partners are *ex-officio* chairmen of this committee, and with them sit eight other members chosen by and out of the *noyau*, five of whom must be workmen, and three clerks or other superior *employés*. The *comité de conciliation* conduct the examination of candidates for admission to the *noyau*. On the death or resignation of a managing partner they nominate his successor for election by the assembled *noyau*, and they alone are authorised to pronounce the definitive dismissal, for misconduct, of a member of the *noyau*, and the consequent forfeiture of all the claims which he may have on the Mutual Aid Society.*
The powers of this body stop short, however, of *executive* functions. The business direction of the house is placed exclusively † in the hands of the two managing partners, who hold half the capital, and undertake personal liability for losses, which does not attach to the workmen except in an indirect manner through their interest in the reserve-fund. In order to render possible the election, as managing partner, of the best qualified man in the house irrespectively of his pecuniary circumstances, it is provided that, on the

---

* So keen is the sense of disgrace incurred by an unworthy appearance before this body when sitting judicially, that men brought to its bar to be thus judged and sentenced by their own comrades have been known to shed tears like children, and be unable to utter a word in their own defence.

† The *noyau*, however, annually elect for one year the foremen (*chefs d'atelier*) from a list proposed by the managing partners.

occurrence of a vacancy, the capital of the outgoing partner shall not be compulsorily withdrawn until the expiration of such a period as shall enable it to be replaced out of the sum accruing to his successor as share in profits from the date of the latter's appointment onward. During this interval, which at the present rate of profits would not exceed three years in the case of the senior, or five in that of the junior partner, interest at five per cent. on the retained capital would be paid to the ex-partner or his representative, but no share of profits.

The conditions of admission to the Mutual Aid Society are membership of the *noyau*, five years of work for the house, good conduct and freedom from any chronic disease. The administration is in the hands of a *conseil de famille*, consisting of a president, six officers annually elected by the whole body of members, and twelve "visitors" chosen by yearly turns from the roll of the Society. These latter, besides taking part during their year of office in the proceedings of the managing council, are charged with very specific and important duties of brotherly kindness towards such members of the Society as, by reason of sickness or distress of any kind, stand in need of its active intervention. The visitors serve only one year at a time; the officers on the contrary are re-eligible. The *conseil de famille* regulates the admission of new members to the Society, the administration of aid during sickness and at death, and the assignment and payment of pensions, life-insurances, etc. It also causes the books of the house to be annually inspected, in order to be able to certify that the share of profits due to the Society has been fully paid over.

It is obvious that the organisation roughly sketched out in the preceding pages must by its very nature put those who co-operate in working it through an invaluable school of practical training in morality and public virtue. To have obtained access to the *noyau* and the Mutual Aid Society by good conduct and active self-improvement, to have discharged the "visitor's" duty in the homes of suffering comrades, to have sat on committees, made and received reports, contributed to important decisions, perhaps even to have been entrusted, as a member of the *comité de conciliation*, with weighty disciplinary powers and attendant responsibilities,—every such step is itself a lesson in self-control, in humanity, in impartial conduct and judicial integrity. The workman in Leclaire's unpretentious foundation shares, in fact, the moral discipline which Mr. Mill has described as attaching to the participation of the private citizen in public functions. "He is called upon to weigh interests not his own; to be guided, in case of conflicting claims, by another rule than his private partialities; to apply at every turn principles and maxims which have for their reason of existence the general good; and he usually finds associated with him in the same work minds more familiarised than his own with these ideas and operations, whose study it will be to supply reasons to his understanding and stimulation to his feeling for the general good." *

With minds expanded and invigorated in this prac-

* *Representative Government*, p. 68.

tical school, the members of Leclaire's house have come to grasp firmly and apply unhesitatingly conclusions which, though no doubt direct consequences of the principle of participation, would hardly be recognised as inseparably bound to it except by minds familiar with at least the elements of political economy.

They know that the more expeditiously work is despatched, the greater will be the amount of business which the house can get through in the course of the year, and the greater the return on labour which will accrue to each individual workman. Accordingly, abandoning the system of organised waste of time which was thought an excellent expedient for thwarting the master under the old system, they work with self-sustained energy during the hours of labour.

They know that if the work executed is always of the very best kind, the reputation of the house and their earnings will remain at the highest point, but that every piece of work badly done tends to drive away its custom and prejudice their own interests. Accordingly the scamping of work and the introduction of inferior or defective materials, in fact every form of trade dishonesty, is sternly discountenanced by the men themselves.

They know that wanton destruction of tools or materials is merely one way of throwing their own money into the sea. Accordingly this proceeding, which has a certain zest about it when thought to be practised to the sole detriment of a non-participating master, is seen in its true character and replaced by a vigilant watch exercised over every article of property belonging to the house.

In these and numberless other ways the feeling of identity of interest which animates the establishment has wonderfully softened the bitter spirit of antagonism towards the possessing class to which no men are more disposed than the Parisian *ouvriers*. The following incident strikingly illustrates the intensity with which this sentiment of solidarity is capable of acting. A workman, dismissed a few years before for having assailed with abuse one of the managing partners, applied in 1876 for readmission to the *noyau*. The formerly offended partner and his colleague readily consented, but in spite of the efforts made by the latter as chairman of the *comité de conciliation*, the other members of that body, on which representatives of the workmen are in a majority, decided unanimously that the former offender should remain permanently excluded from the *noyau*, on the grounds that, having permitted himself to insult a partner of the house, no indulgence ought to be shown him; that the rules must be respected; and that it was better to sacrifice the interest of one man than to compromise the general interest.

M. Charles Robert informed me that, after long experience of the proceedings of the *noyau*, he considered the appointments made by them to have been uniformly good, and to have justified the very great trust reposed in that body by Leclaire. In particular he referred to their selection, at a general meeting and without any official candidature, of a committee for adjudging prizes to the apprentices for progress in technical study, as extremely well managed; great care having been taken to place no one on the committee who was personally connected with any of the competitors.

Of the general moral improvement now manifest throughout the house, M. Marquot, who was private secretary to the founder and has enjoyed the amplest opportunities of watching this progress, spoke to me in the strongest terms. The house-painters were, he said, at the time when Leclaire commenced his efforts on their behalf, notoriously the most dilatory, intemperate, debauched and intractable workmen to be found in Paris. The members of the *noyau*—the "Old Guard" of the house, as Mr. Hall has most happily designated them—are now greatly in request among architects in consequence of their exceptional possession of diametrically opposite qualities.

The introduction of participation by workmen in the profits of employers admits of being recommended on purely economic grounds as a benefit to both the parties concerned. The increased activity of the workman, his greater care of the tools and materials entrusted to him, and the consequent possibility of saving a considerable part of the cost of superintendence, enable profits to be obtained under a participating system which would not accrue under the established routine. If these extra profits were to be wholly divided among those whose labour produced them, the employer would still be as well off as he is under the existing system. But, assuming that he distributes among his workmen only a portion of this fresh fund, and retains the rest himself, both he and they will at the end of the year find their account in the new principle introduced into their business relations.

It was on this tangible ground of mutual advantage that Leclaire by preference took his stand when publicly defending the system incorporated in his house. He constantly insisted that his conduct had been for his own advantage, and that it was better for him to earn a hundred francs and give fifty of them to his workmen than to earn only twenty-five francs and keep them all for himself. "I maintain," he wrote in 1865, "that if I had gone on in the beaten track of routine, I could not have arrived *even by fraudulent means* at a position comparable to that which I have made for myself."

This may be fully admitted as far as concerns the mere stimulation of the workman's energy by the prospect of increased gain; but the most superficial glance at the great institution reared by Leclaire suffices to show that his real aims were of an entirely different order from those of the self-interested speculator with whom, in his anxiety to avoid the dangerous reputation of an innovating visionary, he professed to identify himself. He was at bottom, as M. Robert assured me, and as is indeed evident from many passages in his published writings, an ardent social reformer, passionately desiring the emancipation of the wage-supported classes from the precarious situation in which the present relations between capital and labour hold them bound as though by some inflexible law of nature. It was with an eye consciously fixed on this distant goal that he thought and wrote and laboured in the immediate interests of his own workmen. As was the case with so many of those who have applied genius to philanthropy, the fountain of Leclaire's enthusiasm was essentially religious, though of a kind unconnected with the special dogmas of any particular Christian body. How intensely he held the "great commandment" of Christian morality appears from the following words written in sight of death, when he felt "sincerity" to be "more than ever a duty:"—

I believe in the God who has written in our hearts the law of duty, the law of progress, the law of the sacrifice of one's self for others. I submit myself to his will, I bow before the mysteries of his power and of our destiny. I am the humble disciple of him who has told us to do to others what we would have others do to us, and to love our neighbour as ourselves: it is in this sense that I desire to remain a Christian until my last breath.*

We have seen what one unaided man, imbued with this victorious spirit, was able to contribute towards the solution of the great social problem of our day— how, by bettering the relations between capital and labour, to assure to the toiling masses a self-respecting present and a hopeful future. I cannot believe that this consummation will ever be reached through the conflicts of opposing self-interests; it can only be from "economic science *enlightened by the spirit of the gospel*," † and pointing over the heads of lower antagonisms to a higher unity, that an ultimate solution is to be looked for.

* "Je crois au Dieu qui a écrit dans nos cœurs la loi du devoir, la loi du progrès, la loi du sacrifice de soi-même pour autrui. Je me soumets à sa volonté, je m'incline devant les mystères de sa puissance et de notre destinée. Je suis l'humble disciple de celui qui nous a dit de faire aux autres ce que nous voudrions qu'il nous fût fait, et d'aimer notre prochain comme nous-mêmes; c'est ainsi que je veux rester chrétien jusqu'à mon dernier soupir."

† M. Charles Robert, *La Question Sociale*, p. 43. Paris, Henri Bellaire.

ESSAY II.

PROFIT-SHARING IN INDUSTRY.

(*Nineteenth Century*, May, 1881.)

SOME forty years ago Channing delivered to a Boston audience a course of lectures " On the Elevation of the Working Classes." These lectures possess many conspicuous excellences of thought, feeling and expression, but pre-eminent even among these are the piercing clearness of vision with which the remote goal for a workman's best efforts is descried, and the energetic precision with which it is pointed out in passages such as the following :—

> There is but one elevation for a labourer and for all other men. There are not different kinds of dignity for different orders of men, but one and the same for all. The only elevation of a human being consists in the exercise, growth, energy, of the higher principles and powers of his soul. A bird may be shot upwards to the skies by a foreign power; but it rises, in the true sense of the word, only when it spreads its own wings and soars by its own living power. So a man may be thrust upward into a conspicuous place by outward accidents; but he rises only in so far as he exerts himself and expands his best faculties and ascends by a free effort to a nobler region of thought and

action. Such is the elevation I desire for the labourer, and I desire no other. This elevation is, indeed, to be aided by an improvement in his outward condition, and in turn it greatly improves his outward lot ; and, thus connected, outward good is real and great ; but supposing it to exist in separation from inward growth and life, it would be nothing worth, nor would I raise a finger to promote it.

While, however, Channing saw thus clearly wherein consisted the only real elevation of the working classes, and also recognised the powerful influence exerted by their outward condition on their inner life, he was unable to perceive, save vaguely and dimly, the agencies by which a genuine rise in the labourer's condition was to be brought about. He hoped much from increased temperance, economy, hygienic knowledge, education, reading and clearer development of Christian principle ; but how these vital influences were to be organised as direct consequences of changed industrial relations was a problem the very statement of which would probably have appeared to him visionary and futile.

By a remarkable coincidence, at the very time when Channing was defining in America the spiritual aim to be set before the working classes, Leclaire in Paris was preparing an industrial revolution which, though based at first on purely economic considerations, was destined to bring in its train precisely that moral renovation to which Channing looked forward. I refer, of course, to the principle of participation by workmen in the profits of enterprise.

In the preceding Essay I have described the remarkable chain of associated institutions grouped by Leclaire around this central principle   They constitute a permanent industrial foundation, unique both in the nature of its organisation and in the extent of the benefits, material and moral, which it bestows on its members. This very uniqueness, however, while it attracts public attention in an eminent degree to the Maison Leclaire, is only too likely to discourage imitation of an establishment so elaborately and munificently organised, founded too by an exceptionally situated man of unquestionable genius. The very completeness of the organisation thus tends to obscure the merits of the principle on which it is based. I hope, therefore, to do service by showing that participation in profits, organised on a much less extensive scale and on simpler plans in a large number of industrial and commercial establishments on the Continent, is producing results of the same kind, though not so far-reaching, as those attained by the Maison Leclaire.

In the present Essay, after indicating the principal sources of information in regard to these establishments, I shall describe selected instances of the main types on which participation has been organised in them. The results obtained shall be characterised, as far as practicable, in the words of those who have experienced them. A cursory survey of the ground already covered by participatory operations abroad will then lead to a few closing remarks on the applicability of similar methods in this country.

Of published works on participation by far the most important is that of Dr. Victor Böhmert,* Director of the Royal Statistical Bureau, and Professor of

* *Die Gewinnbetheiligung.* Leipzig, Brockhaus, 1878.

Political Economy at the *Polytechnicum*, at Dresden. It rests on an international investigation of the most extensive kind, carried out with extraordinary industry and perseverance. In describing the systems adopted by individual houses, extracts from regulations, statements of account, indeed all kinds of first-hand information, are abundantly supplied, and the results flowing from the methods adopted are often stated in direct communications made by the masters, and, in a few important cases, also by the men employed.

For the results in Paris alone, the chief authority is a volume by M. Fougerousse,* which includes a number of cases not described by Böhmert.

A further source of trustworthy information is the quarterly *Bulletin*,† published by a French society formed in 1879 in order "to ascertain and make known the different modes of participation actually employed in industry." ‡

It will be readily understood that, besides these comprehensive works, there exists a great mass of separate publications dealing with the organisations of individual houses. These are far too numerous for specification save in a *catalogue raisonné* of such literature.

In selecting the types of participation to be described in this Essay, I have followed a mode of classification introduced by M. Fougerousse, based on the

* *Patrons et Ouvriers de Paris.* Paris, Chaix, 1880.
† *Bulletin de la Société de la Participation aux Bénéfices.* Paris, Chaix.
‡ An account of the work undertaken by this society will be found in the next Essay.

manner in which the workpeople's share in profits is made over to them.

The simplest system is that which distributes this share in ready money at the close of each year's account without making any conditions as to the disposal of the sums so paid over. This mode of proceeding is adopted by but a very limited group of firms, the most important among which is the pianoforte-making establishment of M. Bord,* 52, rue des Poissonniers, Paris, which in 1878 employed about four hundred workmen, and had in June, 1882, completed its fifty thousandth pianoforte. Participation was introduced in 1865, in consequence of a strike, on the following basis. After deduction from the net profits of interest at ten per cent. on M. Bord's capital embarked in the business, the remainder is divided into two parts, one proportional to the amount already drawn as interest on capital by M. Bord, the other to the whole sum paid during the year in wages to the workmen. The former of these two parts goes to M. Bord, the latter is divided among all his *employés* who can show six months' continuous presence in the house up to the day of the annual distribution. The share obtained by each workman is proportional to the sum which he has earned in wages, paid at the full market rate, during the year on which the division of profits is made.

The following table shows the sums paid in bonuses from 1866 to 1882, and the ratios which they bore to annual wages :—

---

* Böhmert, § 35. Fougerousse, p. 67. *Bulletin*, 1882, p. 65. Compare No. 1 of the sets of Regulations in the Appendix to this volume.

Year.	Total of Bonuses to Labour.	Ratio of Bonus to Annual Wages.
	£	
1866	647	9.40 per cent.
1867	1529	17 ,,
1868	1171	12.86 ,,
1869	1891	20 ,,
1870	1886	18 ,,
1871*	—	—
1872	2214	15 ,,
1873	2739	20 ,,
1874	3523	20 ,,
1875	4848	22 ,,
1876	4498	20 ,,
1877	4141	17 ,,
1878	3784	15 ,,
1879	2874	12 ,,
1880	3548	16 ,,
1881	4054	18 ,,
1882	5205	20 ,,

M. Bord has satisfied himself that a good and thrifty employment is made of these annual labour-dividends, and he considers that the effect of the system in attaching the workmen to the house, and its influence on their relations towards their employer, are excellent.†

From the system of immediate distribution, I pass to a diametrically opposite procedure introduced some thirty-three years ago, under the auspices of M. Alfred de Courcy, into one of the most important insurance

* The absence of a bonus for the war-year 1870-71 will surprise no one.

† While these pages are passing through the press I learn, from evidence given on the 19th of June, 1883, before a commission appointed by the French Minister of the Interior, that "seven or eight years ago" M. Bord abandoned his share of the net profits, and in 1882 reduced the interest on his capital to five per cent., so that the workmen now actually enjoy the entire profits of the house. [See *Enquête de la commission extra-parlementaire des associations ouvrières nommée par M. le ministre de l'interieur. Faris. Imprimerie Nationale* 1883. *Vol. II. p.* 220.]

companies of Paris, the *Compagnie d'Assurances Générales.** Five per cent. on the yearly profits realised by the company is allotted to its staff, numbering about two hundred and fifty *employés* of all grades, whose fixed salaries are at least equal to those paid in non-participating insurance offices at Paris. No part of this share in profits is handed over in annual dividends. Each successive payment is capitalised and accumulates at four per cent. compound interest until the beneficiary has completed twenty-five years of work in the house, or sixty-five years of age. At the expiration of this period, he is at liberty either to sink the value of his account in the purchase of a life-annuity in the office, or to invest it in French Government or railway securities. Should he decide on the investment as against the life-insurance, he is allowed to draw only the annual dividends arising from it, as the company retain the stock certificates, and not till after his death abandon their hold on the principal in favour of such persons as he may designate by will to receive it. M. de Courcy, managing director of the company, is well known as the ardent and eloquent advocate of this system of long-deferred, or even only testamentarily transmitted, possession. He insists on the large sums which it has accumulated in comparatively short spaces of time, mentioning the instances of a simple book-keeper in whose name £480 stood to the good after fourteen years of work, a sub-cashier with £800 at the end of twenty-five years, and a superior official with £2600 after a similar period. From the company's point of view

* Böhmert, § 76. Fougerousse, p. 71. Compare No. 2 in Appendix of Regulations.

he alleges the increased permanence, steadiness and assiduity which the deposit account has produced in its staff of *employés*, and instances in particular the redoubled efforts which they willingly make at the seasons of heavy pressure of business. From a letter addressed to me by M. de Courcy, in November, 1880, I translate the following sentences :—

My opinion is more favourable than ever both to the principle of participation and in particular to my system of deferred possession. The institution has now had thirty years of experience, that is to say, of unvarying successes. Each year, by augmenting the account of the *employé*, makes him feel more strongly the advantage of the *deferred* participation. Each year, too, the company appreciates better what it gains in fidelity in return for these sacrifices. My general principle is that there are no thoroughly satisfactory business transactions except those which are satisfactory to both the parties concerned. Experience has justified our institution from each of these points of view. It is excellent for the *employés* and excellent for the company.

From 1850 to 1880 the sum actually *paid over* out of profits to *employés* was £126,437 ; and the whole amount *allotted* down to Christmas 1882 was £203,536.

The share of profits assigned to each man has in some years been as much as twenty-five or thirty per cent. on his salary.

The great majority of participating houses combine the two systems just described : they distribute a part of the workpeople's share of profits in cash bonuses, and invest the remainder for their future benefit. Among establishments thus organised I select for description the firm *Billon et Isaac*,* a joint-stock company manufacturing parts of the mechanism

* Böhmert, § 6.

of musical-boxes at St. Jean near Geneva. The results in that house have been described and commented upon with great fulness of detail by M. Billon in a separate volume, and by members of the working staff in statements communicated to Professor Böhmert and published in his treatise. The system adopted rests on the following exceptionally liberal basis. After deduction of interest on capital and payments to the reserve and maintenance funds, the entire net profits are divided into two equal parts. One of these parts goes to the shareholders and the administration; the other part constitutes the portion assigned to labour. Of this latter sum one-half is annually distributed in cash bonuses proportional to wages earned individually during the year, and the remaining half is invested in the gradual purchase, for the respective beneficiaries, of £4 shares in the company, which carry with them votes at its general meetings. The material results of participation in this house since its first introduction in 1871 appear from the following table, the sums stated in which are given true to the nearest pound:—

Year.	No. of Participants.	Total Average Share allotted to a Workman. £	Ratio of this Share to his entire Annual Wages.
1871-72	103	8	18½ per cent.
1872-73	109	14	28½ ,,
1873-74	92	11	20½ ,,
1874-75	102	12	23½ ,,
1875-76	140	9	17½ ,,
1876-77	98	2	4 ,,
1877-78	82	—*	—* ,,
1878-79	89	4	8 ,,
1879-80	89	6	10 ,,
1880-81	101	8	15 ,,
1881-82	127	10	20 ,,

* Russo-Turkish War.

It will be seen from the above figures that participation has, in this house, had to pass through the ordeal of severe industrial depression directly following on a period of abounding prosperity. This fact should be borne in mind in reading the opinions now to be cited, which were written when the effects of bad trade had already made themselves felt.

The exceptionally complete insight into the working of participation afforded us in the firm Billon et Isaac will, I trust, be held to justify somewhat full quotation from the important judgments on that system expressed by members of the house.

I begin with an extract from a letter written by a workman to Professor Böhmert in 1877 :—

> Since the introduction of participation in profits into this house important changes have become visible. There is no denying the fact that the workman who receives only fixed wages and knows beforehand that however much pains he may take with his work he will not on that account receive an additional farthing from his employers—that this workman becomes more and more negligent and does not bring to bear, as he might do, his full physical and intellectual capacities.
>
> To my great regret I am bound to confess that this kind of thing occurred only too often among ourselves. Such negligence, moreover, does not show itself in the workshop only, it also invades family life. The workman, once sunk to this point, will in the end care as little for the good of his own family as for that of the establishment which employs him. . . . If he has a numerous family to support, it often happens that, in order to avoid seeing his own poverty, or to escape from the complaints of his wife, he seeks a refuge in the pot-house. The inevitable consequence of this conduct is the steadily increasing degradation of this workman and of his family ; similar instances present themselves in abundance at Geneva.
>
> Nevertheless, to remedy such evils is not so difficult a task

as one might suppose. For proof of this it suffices to institute a comparison between the circumstances of the workman in our house before participation in profits with those which we now find there after the introduction of that system.

The undersigned has been working for the last eight years in this factory; he has therefore had sufficient opportunities for observation in this respect, and he can testify that participation in profits has done real wonders in it; one might even say that it has entirely altered the mode of life and habits of the workmen. Formerly, no one thought save of himself and of his individual interests; quarrels about work were nothing out of the common way. Now, on the contrary, all consider themselves as members of one and the same family, and the good of the establishment has become the object of every one's solicitude, because our own personal interest is bound up in it.

It is with pleasure that one remarks how each man strives to fill up his time with conscientious effort to effect the utmost possible saving on the materials, to collect carefully the fallen chips of metal; and how, if one or other now and then is guilty of some negligence, a joking remark from his neighbour suffices to bring him to order again.

If now we cast a glance at the workman's family, we cannot help seeing that there too a notable change for the better has been produced. . . . Those men who formerly spent the chief part of their spare time at the public-house, where they gave vent to such sentiments as the following: "None of us can ever come to anything," have now got hold of quite different ideas. The first payment of shares in profits has laid in their minds the foundation-stone of a new way of looking at things, and awakened hopes for the realisation of which saving is an indispensable condition. One cherishes the hope of purchasing a cottage; another wishes to set up a little shop; a third thinks of accumulating a small sum towards his old age, and, perceiving that the thing may prove possible, takes to staying at home: his wife, overjoyed at this change, strives to make his fireside as pleasant to him as possible, and supports him in the enterprise which he has taken in hand.

The benefits of the system introduced among us are still more manifest in times of commercial crisis like that through which we have passed this winter. For a considerable time we have been reduced to seven hours of labour, and the earnings of a workman with a family on his hands barely sufficed to find food and clothing. Nevertheless one's house-rent had to be paid, and, inasmuch as here nearly all lodgings are paid for three months in advance, more than one of us would have had to sleep with the stars for roof, had not the deposit-account come opportunely to the rescue.

I take the following extracts from a joint opinion signed by seventy of Billon et Isaac's *employés* in the same year:—

Every workman who has become a shareholder and joint proprietor with his employers devotes his utmost attention to the success of the undertaking. The workman, having the same interests as his employers, and perceiving that he is no longer treated like a machine, works with energy and courage: our hearts are warmed and cheered by contact with those of our employers, who are always ready to set us a good example.

Piece-work, premiums, the raising of wages . . . can in nowise replace, for the workman's heart and the master's advantage, participation in profits: under this principle one works with good heart, which is the same thing as saying that one works more and better. It is no longer a mercenary work.

Next hear the opinion of M. Billon in 1877:—

We soon became aware of the good influence which the prospect of sharing in profits exercised on our workmen. An entirely fresh zeal for work, and a lively interest in the house, showed themselves among them; a genuine solidarity was not slow in establishing itself, each man comprehending that all negligence in the performance of his duty was prejudicial alike to his colleagues and to himself. The task of superintendence became easy to us, and we were able thenceforward, without fear of offending any one, to insist on points of detail to which we had hitherto been obliged to shut our eyes. Moreover, the feeling of security with which the attitude of our workmen inspired us, permitted us to give ourselves up wholly to the development of our business. . . . It has often been said to us, "You have not had difficulties with your workmen, thanks to good years. But let an industrial crisis arise, and great will be your embarrassment when you are obliged to dismiss your *employés.*" This contingency, which assuredly we had foreseen when organising participation, has presented itself; and we can say henceforward that it has done nothing but confirm our faith in the principle. . . . The crisis has served to demonstrate that, in bad as in good years, we are better situated in reference to the men than are those who have not applied the principle of participation. As to our workpeople, it has made them understand, better than any arguments could have done, the benefits of obligatory thrift. Those among them who have shared in profits during these five years have received an annual average of twenty per cent. on their wages, so that, if they have laid by the entire fruit of the participation, they possessed at the time of the last division a sum equivalent to one year's wages.*

In reply to a letter of inquiry, M. Billon was good enough to write to me on the 15th of November, 1880, in the following terms :—

You ask me my present opinion on the working of participation in our house. I am happy to tell you that this principle continues to work to our entire satisfaction. . . . After ten years of experience we congratulate ourselves more and more on having adopted it. Its application has to such a degree become ingrained into our modes of doing business that we should not know how to get on without it; the management of an undertaking appears to us no longer possible without this element of justice, harmony, and peace.

After referring to piece-work, premiums, etc., as all good in their places and measures, M. Billon added—

These methods are all inadequate to obtain the complete adhesion of the workman (*l'ouvrier tout entier*); it is only by participation in profits accorded on a suitable scale that his interest in the economic side of an undertaking (care of materials, products, etc.) is thoroughly aroused, and that the sentiment of solidarity is developed and bears its fruits.

* *Participation des Ouvriers aux Bénéfices des Patrons,* par Jean Billon. Genève, H. Georg, 1877, pp. 28, 30, 31.

In a letter dated the 7th of July, 1883, M. Billon wrote to me :—

> I have nothing new to tell you in regard to the practice of participation, and can only confirm my previously expressed opinions.

Before quitting the methods practised in individual houses, I will roughly indicate the amount of progress which the system has as yet made, and the varieties of industry to which it has been successfully applied. Putting together the most recent data, I shall be below the mark in saying that *one hundred* Continental firms are now working on a participatory basis. The principle has been introduced with good results into agriculture ; into the administration of railways, banks and insurance offices ; into iron-smelting, type-founding and cotton-spinning ; into the manufacture of tools, paper, chemicals, lucifer-matches, soap, cardboard and cigarette-papers ; into printing, engraving, cabinet-making, house-painting and plumbing ; into stockbroking, bookselling, the wine trade and haberdashery.

This list does not profess to be anything like complete, but it will probably suffice for the purpose now in view. The establishments which it summarises differ in size and importance as much as in the character of the industry which they pursue, from the paper-mills of M. Laroche-Joubert at Angoulême with their fifteen hundred workmen, to the establishment of M. Lenoir at Paris with its forty house-painters. I may add that the movement is making decided headway, a considerable number of houses having given in their adhesions during the last four years.

The benefits accruing from participation successfully practised may be thus summed up. It furnishes to the workman a supplementary income under circumstances which directly encourage, or even by a gentle compulsion actually enforce, saving; and, by associating him in a very real sense with his employer, it arouses aspirations from which great moral improvement may be confidently anticipated. The employer, besides sharing in whatever surplus profits are realised by the more efficient labour which participation calls forth, obtains the boon of industrial stability and the support of a united corporate feeling elsewhere unknown. Independently of these advantages to the two parties directly concerned, the customer of a participating house finds in its very organisation a guarantee for enhanced excellence of workmanship and rapidity of execution.

On the facts set out in this Essay it seems natural to ask whether there is any reason why a system which is producing abroad results of so much value should not prove equally beneficial if properly introduced among ourselves. It is no sufficient answer to point to half a dozen English experiments in which the system after a few years of trial was finally abandoned, and say that the principle "has been tried and has failed." In order to infer from the abandonment of a system the unsoundness of its central principle, evidence must be forthcoming to show that the evils which led to the failure were necessary consequences of the principle. This has certainly never been proved with respect to the unsuccessful English experiments; and my confident belief is that, in the most conspicuous cases of failure both here and on the Continent, the causes which led to the break-down can be shown to have been extraneous to the principle of participation.

A more satisfactory mode of investigating the adaptability of the system to English circumstances lies in ascertaining, first, what are the conditions under which it promises an economic success, and next, whether those conditions hold to any important extent in this country.

The fund on which participation draws is the surplus profit realised in consequence of the enhanced efficiency of the work done under its stimulating influence. Such extra profit is, therefore, obtainable wherever workmen have it in their power to increase the quantity, improve the quality, or diminish the cost price of their staple of production by more effective exertion, by increased economy in the use of tools and materials, or by a reduction in the costs of superintendence. In other words, the surplus profit realisable will depend on the influence which manual labour is capable of exerting upon production. Evidently, therefore, this influence will be greatest in branches of industry where the skill of the labourer plays the leading part, where the outlay on tools and materials bears a small ratio to the cost of production, and where individual superintendence is difficult and expensive. It will, on the contrary, be least effective in industries where mechanism is the principal agency, where interest on capital fixed in machinery is the chief element of cost price, and where the workmen, assembled in large factories, can be easily and effectively superintended.

Participation would, therefore, be applied with the best prospects of success to such industries as agriculture, mining, building, carpentering, decorating, etc., where wages form a leading element of cost ; while the least promising field would be supplied by cotton-spinning, weaving, and other machine-dominated branches of production. That agriculture offers a peculiarly valuable opening will not be doubted by those who are acquainted with the extraordinary results attained during Mr. John Scott Vandeleur's Irish experiment at Ralahine, in the years 1831–33 where an intelligently planned system of profit-sharing scored a complete local triumph over an acute crisis of agrarian discontent and outrage.*

In coal-mining I am assured on excellent authority that a great amount of preventible waste is occasioned by timber, plates, etc., being carelessly buried under *débris* and thus finally lost. That much time is frittered away, and much material and gear wastefully dealt with, by artisans employed in the house-industries to which I have referred, will not be disputed. It is clear, then, that English workmen have it largely in their power to enhance profits by contributing better and more economical labour. That they will be ready to make the more assiduous efforts involved in such labour as soon as they have thoroughly grasped the motives for increased zeal which participation holds out, appears to me equally certain. If, however, the experiment is to be tried, it is obviously from the employers that the initiative must come. They will, of course, make no trial of the system without a pre-

* See Appendix to Essay V.

liminary study of the methods adopted on the Continent, with regard to which so much trustworthy information has now been accumulated by French and German research. In view, however, of the great results which participation seems to promise in raising masses of the labouring population out of the *prolétaire* or hand-to-mouth class, and thereby drying up a main source of our national pauperism, it is to be hoped that employers of labour, productive or distributive, whether on a large or on a small scale, will consider that a complete examination of the whole subject, undertaken with a direct view to practical action, is urgently called for.

ESSAY III.

PROFIT-SHARING IN INDUSTRY—(*Continued*).

(Manchester Statistical Society, January 10, 1883.)

THE system of remunerating labour which assigns to workmen, over and above full market wages, a share in the profits realised by the concern which employs them, has made on the Continent, and especially in France, an amount of headway little suspected even by the leaders of British industry. It was, therefore, with peculiar pleasure, that I accepted the invitation of your Committee to lay before this Society a group of facts and arguments which I felt, in the existing strained relations between capital and labour, could not but be worthy of attention at the head-quarters of British industry.

My aim during the preparation of the paper now to be read has been :—First to state what steps have been, and are now being, taken in France, with the object of informing public opinion on the results already attained by profit-sharing ; next, to set out somewhat fully the mode in which that system is organised and worked in a particular establishment selected as a model typical instance ; and, in the last place, to state the chief benefits conferred by the system, examine the main objections advanced against it, and say a few words on the question with what prospect of success it might be tried in the productive and distributive industries of this country.

My opening topic, then, is the action taken in France to attract public attention to the principle of profit-sharing.

At a meeting of heads of industrial establishments held in Paris on the 30th of November, 1878, it was decided to form an association having for its object "to facilitate the practical study of the various systems under which workmen participate in profits." The means employed by the Society were to be the formation of a reference-collection of printed and manuscript matter bearing theoretically and practically on profit-sharing, and the publication in quarterly numbers of an annual bulletin* containing some two hundred pages of information on the progress of the participatory movement.

A few passages which I translate from the preface to the first volume of the *Bulletin*, dated the 1st of March, 1879, will show in how thoroughly business-like a spirit this work was taken in hand—

> The Society is resolved to preserve to its studies an absolutely practical character, and in order to give unmistakable expression to this determination, decides to admit to membership in its body none but persons actually engaged in manufacture or commerce. It will doubtless turn to account statements of fact or of opinion which may reach it from any quarter, or which it may find in the writings of publicists and men of science, but according to an article of its statutes it can seek its members

---

* *Bulletin de la Participation aux Bénéfices.* Paris, Chaix.

only among chiefs of industry, that is to say, among men entirely competent each in his own branch, directly interested and continuously responsible, charged with the direction of a more or less numerous body of workmen and therefore, in general, but little accessible to empty theories, rash generalisations or speculative systems. In everything, writes to us one of our Alsatian supporters, who himself practises participation, it is necessary to beware of mere theorists, but especially in social questions, and to make advance in them with the greatest prudence. . . . We admit, as legitimate in such matters, only the experimental method applied with discernment and without hasty and premature conclusions. . . . We expressly disavow all intention of calling forth or sustaining controversies, which are too often barren of result. Our sole aim is to make known to all what has been done by some, and to place trustworthy documents and facts carefully verified in the hands of those, already numerous, industrialists who are seeking with perseverance, but without illusive preconceptions, for efficacious means of conciliation and mutual understanding.

I conceive that after these reassuring explanations the most resolutely "practical" man present may dismiss the idea that the French Participation Society is made up of visionary amateur philanthropists, with heads as soft as their hearts, who ought not to be listened to by men conversant with the stern realities of actual life.

The *Bulletin* has published a mass of valuable information on profit-sharing, the most important part of which consists in textual reproduction of the regulations under which that system is practised in different establishments of repute, chiefly in the French metropolis. It is concurrently bringing out, in an appendix to each number, a French translation of Böhmert's great German work,* originally published in 1878,

* *Die Gewinnbetheiligung.* Leipzig, Brockhaus.

containing particulars of 120 cases of profit-sharing in various countries of the old and new worlds, the materials for which were obtained by a private correspondence of an extent to have utterly daunted a writer of any other nationality.

In France, profit-sharing has recently become a question of official cognisance both in the metropolis and the provinces. A commission was appointed by decree of the Prefect of the Seine, on the 27th of January, 1882, to examine, *inter alia*, "under what conditions it would be possible to require of persons taking contracts for work from the City (of Paris) or the Department (of the Seine) that they should admit their workmen to a share in the profits realised by their undertakings." M. Charles Robert, President of the Participation Society, was summoned to give evidence before this Commission, and requested to procure for its information a formal expression of opinion from the committee of his own society. That committee, after holding two long sittings on the question brought before it, recommended by a large majority of votes that no attempt should be made to enforce participation on the contractors, but that to such of them as should establish that system in their business a special premium should be given on every public contract executed by them in a thoroughly satisfactory manner. On the 2nd of May, 1882, the Commission reported, almost unanimously, in the direction recommended by the committee of the Participation Society.

On the 8th of June, 1882, a committee of the Chamber of Deputies reported on two Bills brought in by M. Ballue and M. Laroche-Joubert respectively, which aimed at a far wider extension of similar measures. The Bill of M. Ballue proposed to enforce participation on all individuals or associations to whom the State, the Departments or the Communes assigned any continuous exclusive rights of possession or use. The measure advocated by M. Laroche-Joubert proposed to apply the same compulsion to all contractors executing work even of the most temporary kind at the cost of these public bodies. I quote a few passages from the Report of the committee on these two Bills, as indicating the point of view taken of profit-sharing in French parliamentary circles :—

> We begin by giving full expression to our colleagues of the feeling of satisfaction with which we see brought before the Chamber proposals touching so closely one of the great questions of our time, the equitable distribution of the produce of labour. Participation by the workman in the profits which he co-operates in producing is one form of association—that as yet ill understood and imperfectly studied lever—the high social importance of which can no longer be overlooked. This application of a great principle has already passed beyond the region of mere theory, and has received in large measure the sanction of experience. . . . Participation, under all the varied forms which it has assumed, can point to brilliant attained results. . . . It would be worthy of the Chamber to have imposed on public adminstrations by legislative enactment the obligation of applying, within the sphere of their own undertakings and of the rights conceded by them, the easy procedure of participation, whose merits no longer require demonstration, and to have thus, on the ground where the State is master, sought to dry up the sources of industrial conflict by introducing arrangements based on justice, which are wiser and more efficacious than measures of repression.*

The Report concludes by recommending that the

* *Bulletin*, 1882, p. 72.

Bills of M. Ballue and of M. Laroche-Joubert be both taken into consideration by the Chamber, inasmuch as the former tends to introduce more widely a social reform already proved to be salutary, while the second, though requiring amendment in respect of the too sweeping terms in which it is couched, also rests on the same solid foundation.

It is obvious that proposals for municipal or state interference between employers and employed require to be, and at Manchester assuredly will be, examined with scrupulous and even jealous care. There will be many shades of opinion on the subject, including that entertained by the minority on the committee of the French Participation Society, who were for rejecting such interference altogether. Profit-sharing, however, ought to be discussed entirely apart from proposals of this kind, which I am far from wishing to raise a discussion upon this evening, and have mentioned only in order to show how considerable a position in the deliberations of leading public bodies the topic of participatory industry has already attained in France.*

Limits of space would render useless an attempt to survey, in a single paper of reasonable length, the whole field of my subject, or even to examine with satisfactory fulness the organisations of more than one profit-sharing house. It may perhaps be expected by some of my hearers who are familiar with the history of participation that, this being so, I should almost of necessity select as my type-instance the

* A volume just issued by order of the Minister of the Interior containing more than 500 pages of evidence on Profit-Sharing, taken before his commission of inquiry on workmen's associations, affords a further indication to the same effect. (See *ante*, p. 31, note.)

Maison Leclaire, which, by reason of priority in date, elaborateness of organisation and grandeur of attained results, occupies an absolutely unique position.

There are, however, I conceive, valid reasons which dictate a different choice. The *Maison Leclaire* is neither a private firm nor even a joint-stock undertaking, but a permanent Foundation, holding towards other industrial establishments the position which endowed places of education like Eton or Winchester occupy when compared with schools supported only by the funds of individuals or of private associations. Now, my present object is to describe—not an institution of an unique and scarcely reproducible kind—but a profit-sharing house of the best type which, like other firms, has only private financial legs to stand upon. I will, therefore, bespeak your attention to a great Parisian printing, publishing and bookselling house—the *Maison Chaix**—which supplies literature to the French railway bookstalls, and has been, though but inadequately, described as Bradshaw and the Right Hon. W. H. Smith rolled into one. I have selected this firm for description, partly because of the admirable manner in which participation is organised and worked in it, and partly because a visit paid in the spring of last year justifies my speaking of its arrangements with the confidence bred of even slight personal inspection.

Previously to 1872 the house was managed on the ordinary system. Profit-sharing commenced from the 1st of January of that year. M. Chaix announced his intention of assigning to his regularly employed

* Compare No. 3 in Appendix of Regulations.

staff of workmen and clerks, under specified conditions as to length of previous service, a share in the net profits realised by the house—the amount of such share to be independently fixed in each successive year by M. Chaix himself. The sum thus allotted was to be divided into three equal parts, to be separately dealt with as follows:—

The first to be handed over each year in cash. The second to be paid to a provident and pension fund. The third to be likewise paid to this fund, but to be available for beneficiaries only on attaining sixty years of age, or after twenty years of uninterrupted work in the house.

The amount constituting the cash bonus was to be distributed among the individual recipients in proportion to the sums which they had respectively received in wages or salaries during the year for which the distribution took place. All *employés* who could show three years of continuous presence in the house were on the 1st of January, 1872, admitted as participants, but for the future there were added two other conditions, viz. proved competence and zeal in their calling, and a written application for admission handed in to M. Chaix.

The first third-part of the share in profits having been handed over in ready money to the participants, the second was to be divided into like portions, and each paid into a savings account opened in the name of its recipient. The house undertook to add to the sums standing in these accounts yearly interest at the rate of four per cent. as long as they remained in its custody. The accumulated capital thence resulting could be claimed by a participant either on completing sixty years of age or twenty years of work for the house, or on quitting its service, for whatever reason, at an earlier period.

The remaining third-part of the share in profits was to be treated like the second, and also to receive interest at four per cent., but its accumulations were only to reach beneficiaries on their definite retirement after having attained the full term of years or of service stated above,* and the families of such participants as should die while on active work for the house prior to the completion of that term.

The objects which M. Chaix had in view when making these arrangements cannot be better expressed than in the following words of his own:—

> In giving to the *personnel* of his establishment an interest in the annual profits, M. Chaix proposed to himself a twofold object.
>
> He desired, in the first place, to improve the present material condition of the workmen, workwomen and clerks of the house, by enabling them to draw each year a sum entirely distinct from their wages or salaries; and next, to create for them in the future a capital of which they might dispose, either for their own profit or for that of their families.
>
> M. Chaix thinks that these new arrangements ought to result in the establishment of a moral and material bond of union between the house and those employed in it, of such a kind that the house may derive an advantage from it in respect of the thorough and rapid execution of work.†

Since the establishment of profit-sharing in 1872, the reports presented by the committee of manage-

---

* Accounts lapsing through the non-fulfilment of these conditions were to be distributed among the accounts of the remaining participants in proportion to the sums already standing in them.

† This and the following quotations from statements made by M. Chaix are taken from printed reports annually issued by the house.

ment, and the addresses delivered by M. Chaix at each successive annual meeting of the participating workmen, afford detailed evidence of the steadily increasing success which has attended the working of the system just described. I propose to set out very summarily the material and moral results thus attained.

The number of persons admitted as participants at the inauguration of the system was 117. There have subsequently been admitted 437, bringing the total up to 554. If from this number be deducted those who have taken their retirement, died or quitted the house, there remained 354 as the number of participants on the books on the 1st of January, 1883.

M. Chaix has annually assigned to his *employés* fifteen per cent. of the net profits realised. The total sum thus allotted during the ten years from 1872 to 1881 was £25,991, of which £6,242 was paid over in cash bonuses. The share in profits allotted in each year averaged seven and a half per cent. on the total of wages and salaries—*i.e.* two and a half per cent. handed over in ready money, and five per cent. laid up for future accumulation. The accounts standing in the names of participants of various grades in the house were, on the 31st of December, 1881, as follows:—

Number of accounts of £300 and upwards		...	5
,,	,, from £200 to £300	...	9
,,	,, ,, £100 to £200	...	39
,,	,, ,, £80 to £100	...	8
,,	,, ,, £60 to £80	...	19
,,	,, ,, £40 to £60	...	32
,,	,, ,, £20 to £40	...	58
,,	,, of £20 and under	...	164
			334

The pecuniary results attained in 1882 contrasted very unfavourably with those of the previous years. Fifteen per cent. on the net profits realised yielded to each participant only one and a half per cent. on his year's wages. This unsatisfactory state of things is attributed by M. Chaix to industrial depression, combined with intensified competition in the printing trade, especially that exerted by the *Imprimerie Nationale*, a State printing establishment armed with monopolistic claims upon all the public departments, and supported out of general taxation, so that it is able to combat private firms with resources to which its competitors are themselves obliged to contribute.

At the opening of 1883 the 354 participants formed about one-third of the total number of *employés*. A greater ratio would, doubtless, have been shown but for the fact that in 1881 the number of persons employed by the house was very largely increased, and that a considerable proportion of them had therefore not yet had time to complete the period of probation required to qualify them as participants.

A few extracts translated from M. Chaix's addresses to the annual meetings will best show his opinion of the moral benefits resulting from the system.

On the 5th of April, 1874, he said :—

> I have ascertained with satisfaction that the introduction of profit-sharing has, as I hoped it would do, developed the zeal of those interested in it : each one takes more interest in the work assigned to him and executes it better and more expeditiously.

On the 28th of March, 1875, M. Chaix said :—

> If there be a spectacle which should satisfy the friends of social peace, it is assuredly that presented by the industrial

family of this establishment, when, at the completion of the year's work, it is gathered together in order to learn the results of our joint exertions, and the amount of its allotted share in the profits realised. No institution is, indeed, better adapted to draw close the bonds which unite you to the house, and to inspire you with confidence in the future, than participation which has enabled me to constitute for your benefit, not only certain immediate advantages, but also an economised capital which has for some among you already reached important dimensions.

The address of the 13th of April, 1879, contains the following passage :—

In what concerns the execution of work in the workshops and in the offices, I find around me such an amount of willing zeal that I give the main credit for this excellent state of things to profit-sharing, and congratulate myself more and more on having set that principle working in the house.

At the meeting on the 17th of April, 1881, M. Chaix, after rapidly sketching the progress made in public estimation by participatory industry, continued as follows :—

In one word, economical theory and practice have henceforth to reckon with this new system, and I am profoundly convinced that if those who are indifferent or hesitating could be present when the account of a participant of some standing is closed, they would—on witnessing the satisfaction with which the old workman or his widow receives his capitalised property —comprehend the extent of the service rendered to the labouring class by this patient accumulation of savings and resolve to practise it themselves. Certainly participation is no universal panacea, nor the last word of social well-being, but I do not hesitate to affirm that it constitutes an incontestible advance upon the existing system of the organisation of labour. You know what the old trade guilds were ; you know how firm a bond united all their members and kept actual misery from the workman's door. But these guilds, whatever the good with which they may justly be credited, were a hindrance to freedom of labour. . . . They were accordingly abolished, like all other privileged institutions, and the absolute independence of the workman was proclaimed. This independence created a new evil, worse perhaps than the abolished privilege; it created the isolation of the workman, and the antagonism between capital and labour. Among all the systems which have been devised in order to restore the old union of interests without impairing the liberties newly conquered, participation is assuredly one of the best. . . . It is possible that experience may suggest in the future a different method of organising participation from that adopted in our house. But be this method what it may, it will, I entertain no doubt, lead to an understanding between capital and labour, to a reign of peace and harmony under which, without encroaching on the rights of property, it will be possible to give to intelligence, to activity and to devotion their legitimate share. Then this disastrous schism and huge isolation which have existed in industrial society for the last ninety years will hasten to their close. This just balance of interests and rights will render the workshop more moral, while instruction, abundantly given in technical schools, will raise the intellectual level of our young workmen. Without losing aught of our liberties, we shall thus recover the harmony from which the old trade guilds drew their strength.

During a visit paid to the *Maison Chaix*, in the spring of 1882, I had long conversations not only with the chief of the establishment, but with heads of departments, foremen and other members of the house. As far as I could learn, the participatory principle was held in the utmost esteem, and its application had proved free from any serious difficulty. The only complaint I heard came from an old foreman who was not quite satisfied with the rate at which the principle was producing the moral results he expected from it.

Before closing this necessarily very inadequate

account of a model establishment, I wish to say a word or two on an institution existing within it which, though to be found in perhaps only two or three other participating houses, has an important bearing on the future welfare and progress of profit-sharing.

M. Chaix has organised for the apprentices of his house an *école professionnelle*, or course of special instruction destined to make them thoroughly competent artificers, well-informed men and useful members of society. The theoretical portion of the course is given in class-rooms specially devoted to the purpose by instructors who are themselves superior *employés* or foremen of the house, or, in some few cases, professional teachers imported from without. The programme of subjects to be studied by the compositor-apprentices falls into three divisions. The first comprises the language, history and geography of France, arithmetic and elementary geometry in special relation to typographical problems, and book-keeping. The second division embraces the whole subject of typography technically treated, together with notions of lithography and engraving, and some acquaintance, for professional purposes, with Latin, Greek, German and English, printed and written.

The third division sets out with considerable fulness the history of printing and of printed books, and, by supplying detailed biographical notices, encourages the future compositor to dwell with a feeling of corporate pride on the lives of those by whom the great and beneficent steps in the art of printing were made, and who constitute in a sense his spiritual ancestry.

The programme closes with some elements of

Physics and Chemistry in their leading applications, and a careful selection of such parts of Political Economy and Law as bear directly on the industrial welfare of the workman, and on his rights and duties as a citizen.

The house not only defrays the entire cost of maintaining the apprentice school, but credits each pupil with ten centimes for each satisfactory attendance at it. The sum thus accruing to an apprentice is paid over to him each month as pocket-money.

An informality accidentally committed at the first establishment of the *école professionnelle* attracted to it the special notice of the Minister of Public Instruction. In France, as is well known, a preliminary Government authorisation is required from every one who proposes to open a school. M. Chaix seems to have thought this provision not intended to include so strictly internal and almost domestic a system of tuition as that just described. At any rate he started his courses without informing the Government, and worked away at them for some time without any misgivings as to the consequences of this omission. At last a friend arrived in great consternation to tell him that he had already rendered himself liable to a heavy fine, and that the best thing he could do was to shut up his school forthwith, and trust to the affair not reaching the ears of the Government. M. Chaix took the precisely opposite course of writing straight to the Minister of Public Instruction, explaining frankly what had occurred, and asking for a Bill of Indemnity. M. Duruy, then head of the Education Department, at once paid a visit to the *Maison Chaix*, and personally inspected the *école professionnelle*, of which he expressed a warm approval. On being informed by M. Chaix that the apprentices were allowed ten centimes for every attendance, the Minister laughed very heartily, and said, " Why, people are constantly attacking me for my advocacy of *gratuitous* education, and here are you outdoing me by paying your pupils for consenting to be taught."

This visit was soon followed by a present of some handsome prizes for the best pupils of the school, from the Minister of Public Instruction.

When I was at the *Maison Chaix* I not only saw the apprentice-school in active operation and satisfied myself as to the excellence of the work done both by teachers and learners, but asked every man whom I came across in the house his opinion on the results of the institution and on the nature of its organisation. The unanimous reply was, that between two lads equally situated in other respects, one of whom had served his apprenticeship under M. Chaix, and the other in a house conducted according to the ordinary routine, *no comparison at all was possible.* The one was a practically and theoretically accoutred and accomplished workman. The other was a mere rule-of-thumb practitioner, who knew nothing thoroughly, and whose intelligence had received no cultivation whatever. There was equal unanimity in holding that by no other system than a course of instruction given in the house itself, and exclusively controlled by the executive of the firm, could results be looked for at all approaching those attained in the *Maison Chaix*.

The following inherent advantages of such a system were, among others, urged in support of this view :—

1. The practical instruction of the apprentices at the machines can be given at hours when the foremen and the machines are most at liberty ; at seasons of unusual pressure these hours can be shifted about at pleasure, or some theoretical branch of study temporarily substituted for the technical instruction, until such time as diminished pressure shall allow this subject to be resumed and brought up to its proper position in the course.

2. Due regard can be had to modes of technical procedure special to the establishment, which in a leading house are neither few nor unimportant.

3. The knowledge gained by the foremen of the character and habits of the apprentices during their hours of ordinary industrial work is of great value when communicated to their teachers in the school.

4. The direct control exerted over the school by the head of the house enables him to form, in the most natural way, permanent friendly relations with his future workmen.

In passing at this point from a veritable *maison d'élite* whose institutions would well repay far more detailed study, I may state a fact which is in itself the strongest testimonial in favour of the participatory principle. In the year 1881, the establishment ceased to be a private firm and was turned into a joint-stock company. The Directors of the new undertaking were unanimously in favour of retaining the principle of participation, administered on the liberal scale previously adopted by the private firm, and the general meeting of shareholders adopted, likewise with absolute unanimity, a resolution carrying that recommendation into effect.

[A passage containing a summary of results attained in different participatory undertakings, which found a place at this point in the paper as read at Manchester, is omitted, as fuller details in respect of all of them are given elsewhere in this volume.]

I quit at this point the specification of results attained in particular houses, in order to take a rapid survey of the benefits, both to employers and employed, which have been generally found to follow the introduction of well considered and wisely administered schemes of industrial profit-sharing. It will be advisable to notice concurrently a few facts of familiar observation on which the system before us, regarded from a purely economical point of view, will be seen to be securely based. I may perhaps most conveniently begin with these latter.

Two equally capable and energetic men, one of whom is working on his own account and the other performing at fixed wages services which have for their object the enrichment of an employer, notoriously present two very different standards of activity. The former is full of enterprise and alacrity. The latter is wont to be slack and unaspiring and disinclined to make any effort bodily or mental not included in the average standard of performance recognised by his fellows. Where piecework prevails, the above remark ceases to be applicable as far as mere quantity of production is concerned; but the contrast remains as great as ever in respect of the alertness of eye and brain to avoid waste of materials and injury to plant and tools, to suggest reforms in current technical procedure, to improve quality, and, generally speaking, to attain an enhanced commercial result by other methods than piling up a maximum of such work as will only just pass the scrutiny of the examiner appointed to check it. In short, full exertion of bodily and mental powers is obtainable only from men whose own interests are fully engaged in the result of the work to be performed.

This being so, it may reasonably be argued that the unsatisfactory quality of industrial work now so generally complained of is due to the fact that the existing organisation of labour makes no provision for enlisting the workman's active zeal on the side of the ultimate returns to industrial undertakings. That workmen could by applying more zealous labour exert an effective influence in the direction of enhanced profits is, in most branches of production, undisputed and indisputable. The main openings for such influence may be roughly summed up under the four following heads :—

1. Increased production due to the cessation of all deliberate waste of time during the hours of work.

2. Diminution in costs of superintendence, much of which could be dispensed with if it were no longer necessary to extort work by the fear of detected idling and consequent dismissal.

3. Saving to be effected by more thrifty and thoughtful handling of materials, machinery and appliances of all kinds.

4. Improvement in quality of production, due not only to bettered individual work, but also to advances in technical procedure suggested by the ingenuity of the artificer brought to bear fruitfully upon the facts of his daily experience.

Manifestly, then, if the zeal of the workman could

be adequately aroused to call forth sustained labour of this zealous type, enhanced profits would accrue to those industrial establishments which were fortunate enough to secure its services. Such establishments would, therefore, be in a position to allot a share in profits to their *employés* without necessarily making any pecuniary sacrifice themselves. We have here the *à priori* justification of profit-sharing viewed from an exclusively economic standpoint—the expectation, namely, that more efficient labour will be called forth, and thus new profits secured which would not accrue under systems where the workman was not directly interested in the final results of enterprise. It is most important to bear constantly in mind when profit-sharing is being discussed that the system, far from being a scheme for enriching workmen out of the pockets of their employers, has at its command potential energies capable of opening an entirely new source of profits, and so of creating the fund which it proposes to distribute.

In addition to being a source of direct pecuniary advantage, profit-sharing brings about manifold beneficial results, which I take the liberty of laying before this Society in the terms in which I described them to the Economy and Trade Section of the Social Science Association in October, 1881.

" It introduces into the relations between employers and employed a remarkable and sorely needed stability and peace. Violent fluctuations in the rate of wages are avoided, inasmuch as the workmen, knowing that at the end of the year they will receive their appointed share of whatever prosperity has in the course of it visited the concern which employs them, no longer see occasion to demand a rise of wages whenever heavy orders are known to have come in. A strike, too, will be far less readily resorted to by men who have come to perceive that such a measure not only stops their wages for the time being, but inflicts a further injury on them by curtailing the profits divisible at the year's end.

"The strong corporate feeling which prevails in a well organised participating house is also a great support to its managing head. He no longer has to contend with the class spirit which, under the ordinary conditions of remuneration, so uniformly bands together the workmen against their employer. On the contrary, he finds himself, in any act of necessary severity, backed up by the public opinion of the workshop which, under the salutary teaching of participation, has learned that a lazy, dissolute or dishonest artificer is as much a source of loss to his comrades as to his employer. This educational power, inherent in the system, leads to many beneficial results. It encourages practical study of the economic conditions under which profits are realisable. It sets the most intelligent workmen on the alert for possible improvements by which more produce can be turned out, or fresh economies effected. M. Chaix tells how, soon after he had introduced profit-sharing into his house, two of his compositors proposed that their frames should be put closer together so that they might be able to set up type by the light of a single lamp, and thus avoid the waste involved in burning two. He also found some of his clerks practising a rather overstrained economy by sending out proofsheets in soiled envelopes which had already passed through the post.

"To the workman the allotment of his share in profits in a sum entirely distinct from his wages affords a valuable encouragement to saving. Enquiries made in important houses where annual cash distribution takes place have shown that the sums thus received have been, for the most part, either placed in sound investments or spent in sensible ways not involving a raised standard of outlay and a consequent increase in the price of commodities. In houses which retain the share in profits of their *employés* for a given number of years, sums relatively very considerable have been accumulated at compound interest to the credit of the beneficiaries. The advantage to a working man of possessing a small capital on which to fall back when his powers of self-support are checked by illness, or exhausted in old age, is too manifest to need insisting on."

More important than even these material benefits is the inspiriting consciousness felt by the workman that he is no longer treated as if he were a mere productive machine, but has become, in a real though restricted sense, a co-partner with his employer. The workpeople of a factory at Geneva have given animated expression to this feeling;* and I know of an instance in which a clerk employed in an English house where, in addition to a fixed salary, he received a share in profits, refused to quit its service for a more lucrative post remunerated by fixed salary only, assign-

* See *ante*, p. 37.

ing as his reason that he preferred the higher status involved in participation to larger total earnings obtained at the cost of relinquishing it.

It is now time that I should state, and briefly reply to, the principal objections which have been alleged against the system described in this paper. The instances which I am about to give embody the strongest adverse arguments with which I am acquainted.

Objection 1.—It is unjust that workmen should share in *profits* unless they are willing and able to share in *losses* when these occur. If they receive an amount additional to wages in a good year when a profit has been realised, they ought to be prepared to pay back something out of wages in a bad year when a loss has been incurred. Participation, as it involves no such liability on the workman's part, is necessarily a one-sided and therefore an essentially unjust arrangement.

Reply.—It is not true, as this objection takes for granted, that workmen contribute nothing towards losses. We have seen that under successful participation additional profits, due to the more zealous efforts of the workpeople, are realised. A part only of this surplus is, as a rule, allotted to labour. The remainder which goes into the pocket of the employer, may, since it is exclusively produced by the workmen, be with strict propriety regarded as their contribution towards his future losses in bad years. Further, it must be remembered that participating workmen incur a positive loss whenever there are no profits to divide—the loss, namely, of all the extra care and exertion which they have expended in the prospect of a share in profits to accrue at the year's end.*

Objection 2.—If workmen are once permitted to share in the profits of a concern, they will presently insist on overhauling its books, and even on thrusting themselves into its business management.

Reply.—This objection is one of a whole group founded on the assumption that working men are, as a class, incurably obstinate and utterly unreasonable beings. There have undoubtedly been a few isolated cases where the introduction of profit-sharing has been followed by so arrogant and insupportable an attitude on the part of the men admitted to it, as to compel the withdrawal of the system. But there is ample evidence to show that only under very exceptional circumstances have such results been encountered. No tendency to encroachment has as yet shown itself in the best participating houses, and a foreman at the *Maison Chaix*, to whom I mentioned the objection to the system felt on this ground by some employers, characterised such fears as destitute of all solid foundation. In order, however, to deal quite frankly with the objection in hand, I may express my personal conviction that in proportion as participating workmen feel themselves qualified by improved general education and more thorough technical knowledge to exert some share of influence on the management of the concern in which their own interests are bound up, they will gradually acquire the power of exerting that influence. I cannot see how the advantage of such

---

* In some houses a reserve-fund maintained out of profits enables workmen to share *directly* in losses.

co-operation of individual intelligences, each within the sphere of its special competence, can possibly be denied, unless on the assumption that the employer's brain is so complete a storehouse of every known fact and of every practicable device that no contribution from the circle of his workmen could have for him a shred of novelty or of suggestiveness.

Objection 3.—In years when no profits are made the workmen will consider themselves defrauded of what is their due, and will regard their employer as an actual defaulter.

Reply.—This is another specimen of the objections based on the assumed irrationality of the working classes. The probabilities are, however, the other way, inasmuch as the stimulated intelligence of participating workmen is far more likely to guide them to a just judgment as to the real causes of industrial want of success than is the torpid indifference bred, among non-participating workmen, by exclusion from all share in the fortunes of the house by which they are employed. This view is confirmed by the fact that, in a house at Geneva, where the badness of trade in the year of the Russo-Turkish War forbade the division of any profit, the result, so far from producing reclamations on the side of the workmen, drew from them only the sensible remark that they were better off than their fellows in other houses in a good year, and had as high wages as they in a bad one, so that on the whole they had reason to be well satisfied with their position.*

Objection 4.—It may be very disadvantageous to a

---

* See *ante*, p. 37.

concern if the rate of profits which it is making becomes publicly known. Under some systems of participation, information from which the rate of profits can be immediately calculated is actually published each year, and in most cases it could be very approximately estimated. Profit-sharing is therefore unfavourable to commercial success, and places houses which adopt it under a distinct disadvantage.

Reply.—It is, no doubt, advantageous to a branch of trade, or individual house in that branch, which is realising an exceptionally high rate of profits to keep the fact secret, because, were it to become generally known, capital might be attracted into the business from other investments, and profits be reduced by the increased competition thence arising. It is, therefore, not improbable that employers having capital invested in a concern which brings them an exceptional rate of interest, may, if they are led solely by the desire to retain those profits at their existing level, think it best to avoid incurring whatever publicity attaches to a participating system, though that publicity is not necessarily so considerable or inevitable as the objection assumes. Still, subject to this limitation, the objection has a certain validity. The branches of industry to which it applies are, however, by the nature of the case, only a small minority compared to the great mass of business undertakings which realise only the average rate of profits. These considerations suffice to show that the publicity attendant upon participation, even though it were as complete as some very competent advocates of the system think it ought to be, constitutes no real obstacle to the general adoption of profit-sharing, but only a hindrance to its application in certain exceptional cases.

In estimating the comparative force of the above objections and replies, you will be helped by knowing on which side of the question at issue is to be found the more practically experienced, and therefore the more trustworthy, body of opinion. This piece of information cannot be given with more authority than in the following words in which Professor Böhmert sums up a very full examination of the opposing arguments :—

> Most of the judgments pronounced against participation in profits emanate from men of business who have either never tried the system at all, or else only to an inadequate extent or for too short a time. The unfavourable judgments upon it coming from workmen originate likewise in circles possessing no knowledge derived from actual experience. On the other hand, it is precisely from those employers who have most thoroughly developed the system that we receive decidedly favourable judgments and experiences. . . . The actually participating workmen likewise communicate their approval of the system in the liveliest terms.—Vol. i. pp. 215, 216.

When results so considerable in themselves and so far-reaching in their probable consequences as those described in the present paper are being daily realised on the other side of the Channel, it seems natural to ask of a Society like your own, which unites theoretical and practical qualifications for forming a trustworthy judgment, the following question :—Why should a system which has achieved such remarkable and eminently desirable results in France, fail to confer like benefits upon English houses which should introduce it with equal hopefulness, organise it with equal forethought and administer it with equal wisdom ? On the subsidiary technical question, to what extent it is in the power of operatives employed in such industries as those of Manchester to enhance profits by supplying more zealous work, I am not competent to enter. At mixed conferences where the point has been mooted, I have noticed that the employers present spoke of this influence of labour on profits as likely to be insignificant, while the workmen, on the contrary, expressed the conviction that it would be very considerable.

I will, however, refer to one very important element in the question, with which an outsider may legitimately concern himself,—the probable attitude towards profit-sharing of English trades unions. It is well known that in France such societies are far less powerful, wealthy and militantly organised than in this country. Thoroughgoing opponents of trades unions will doubtless contend that the leaders of those bodies in England will dislike any scheme tending to identify the interests of employers and employed, and do their utmost to frustrate it. Those who argue thus may, I admit, find a certain amount of support for their view in the action of the Miners' Union which led to the abandonment by Messrs. Briggs and Co. of the most celebrated participatory experiment ever made in England—that tried at the Whitwood Collieries near Normanton, Yorkshire, where profit-sharing, introduced in 1865, was withdrawn by a vote of the shareholders early in 1875.*

Nevertheless, in the face of whatever force there

* See *post*, pp. 117-132.

may be in such allegations, I maintain that participation in profits gives all that rational trades unionism contends for, and that the union leaders are more likely to welcome than to repel any genuine attempt to introduce it.

The system, by its very nature, secures to the workmen at each year's end a share in whatever increased prosperity may, in the course of it, visit the house by which they are employed. Participation, therefore, effects by a continuous and almost self-acting process exactly what trades unionism strives to attain by comparatively ill-informed external pressure involving social friction by which much valuable industrial force is, as in a badly constructed machine, wasted by being turned into heat. If an altered system of remunerating labour promises to confer spontaneously what trades unions have hitherto attempted to exact by coercive measures, what reason is there for assuming that the admittedly able men at the head of those organisations will look on the new system with feelings of hostility?

I am in a position to produce distinct statements from men of authority and influence among trades unionists explicitly disavowing such hostility.

Mr. Burt, M.P. for Morpeth, wrote to me in February, 1880:—

> I am glad you are carrying on your efforts in favour of co-partnership, or, as you well express it, participation by the labourer in the profits. I quite agree with your views, and wish you every success.

The two following opinions were given during a discussion on profit-sharing at the Society of Arts in the same month and year: Mr. George Howell said "he could not conceive for one moment that there was any objection to the scheme being tried anywhere, or that any well-organised trade union would raise any objection to it." Mr. Lloyd Jones said "he wished to correct a statement which had been made, that the trades unionists of the country were averse to proposals for the participation of labour in profits. . . . He knew all the leaders in every branch of industry where trade unionism existed, and he did not know of a single case of hostility to such a scheme."

Assuming that economic conditions are favourable, and trades unions not unfriendly, is there any other essential requisite for a participatory success of the kind described in this paper? I believe there is, and that it consists in mutual confidence between employer and employed. The workmen of a house must feel assured that its chief, when introducing these altered industrial relations, is not merely or mainly led by self-interest, but has their material and moral elevation at heart, and intends to be personally at hand with counsel, suggestion and active co-operation, in order to secure from the participatory system the full benefits which it has elsewhere been the means of conferring on the working classes. The head of the house on his side must be able to rely on the workmen for the zealous, sustained and concerted efforts on which the efficacy of the whole system depends.

Of course I am far from meaning to imply that the mutual confidence of which I have spoken must be present at the outset in a developed condition. The very mission of profit-sharing is to unfold, educate and confirm it. Still, it must be present in germ; there must be some willingness on both sides to lay aside the suspicions of the past, and give each other credit in the future for good and unselfish intentions.

Were this feeling entirely absent, or the system even introduced in an atmosphere of determined mutual mistrust, its chance of success would manifestly be most seriously reduced.

Disclaiming all desire to assume a hortatory attitude towards men far more competent than I am to decide the question whether the time has now come for giving participation a thorough trial in British industry, I conclude my paper by placing before you the opinions of two distinguished political economists.

The late W. Stanley Jevons, formerly Professor of Political Economy in Owens College, Manchester, wrote as follows in an excellent volume—*The State in Relation to Labour*, published only last spring,* and therefore containing his very latest judgment:—

> The present doctrine is that the workman's interests are linked to those of other workmen, and the employer's interests to those of other employers. Eventually it will be seen that industrial divisions should be vertical, not horizontal. The workman's interests should be bound up with those of his employer, and should be pitted in fair competition against those of other workmen and employers. Then there would be no arbitrary rates of wages, no organised strikes, no long disputes rendering business uncertain and hazardous. The best workman would seek the best master, and the best master the best workman. Zeal to produce the best and cheapest and most abundant goods would take the place of zeal in obstructive organisation.†

---

* In the series "The English Citizen:" Macmillan and Co.
† p. 145.

The opinion to be next quoted is that of a political economist belonging to a school opposed on many points of importance to that of which Professor Jevons was so distinguished a member and exponent.

The Postmaster-General, Mr. Fawcett, wrote as follows in his work on Pauperism, published in 1871 :—

> It is vain to expect any marked improvement in the general economic condition of the country, as long as the production of wealth involves a keen conflict of opposing pecuniary interests. The forces which ten men can exert may be completely neutralised, if they are so arranged to contend against, instead of assisting, each other. Similarly, the efficiency of capital and labour must be most seriously impaired, when, instead of representing two agents assisting each other to secure a common object, they spend a considerable portion of their strength in an internecine contest. All experience shows that there can be no hope of introducing more harmonious relations, unless employers and employed are both made to feel that they have an immediate and direct interest in the success of the work in which they are engaged.*

I am authorised by Mr. Fawcett to say that he is prepared to repeat, if possible with even stronger emphasis, the favourable opinion on industrial participation expressed in the volume from which I have just quoted. In a letter written to me during a convalescence which the whole country has watched with heartfelt joy and thankfulness, Mr. Fawcett gives me permission to say that, in the last conversation we had together before his illness, he remarked that "the more he thought of the question of profit-sharing, the greater was the importance which he attributed to the extension of the principle."

* Macmillan and Co., p. 164.

The heavy demand which I have made on your attention is now at an end. We have seen that profit-sharing possesses a substantial basis in economical theory, and is in France conspicuously supported by the results of experience. It remains that those with whom rests the initiative among ourselves resolve to give it the trial which seems no more than its due.

ESSAY IV.

PROFIT-SHARING IN THE PARIS AND ORLEANS RAILWAY COMPANY.

(This Essay is mainly an abridged translation from the *Bulletin de la Participation* for 1881, pp. 181–208.)

THE Paris and Orleans Railway Company have, from 1844 down to the present time, annually assigned a share in profits to their permanent staff of *employés* of every grade.

The principles on which the individual distribution of this share took place have been repeatedly modified, as will be seen from the following summary of events.

To M. François Bartholony,[*] late Chairman of the Board of Directors, belongs the honour of having, in 1844, suggested to his colleagues the idea of associating the *employés* of the Company in its profits. A committee appointed to examine this suggestion having reported in its favour, a general meeting of the shareholders, on the unanimous recommendation

[*] M. Bartholony died on the 9th of June, 1881, aged eighty-six years, after having held the chairmanship for more than forty years.

of the Directors, enacted an additional statute worded as follows:—

After the payment of outgoings and the assignment of eight per cent. to the shareholders, there shall be deducted, if circumstances permit, fifteen per cent. on the remaining annual returns, to be distributed by the Board of Directors among the *employés* of the Company on principles to be determined by a regulation which shall be submitted for the approval of the next general meeting.

The regulation thus referred to was approved in general meeting in 1845. Under its terms the Company's officials and *employés* of all grades were divided into three classes.

The first class was composed of the Directors and the Engineers. Each of these was to receive for every thousand francs (£40) of his annual salary, $\frac{1}{300}$th of the distributable amount.

The second class contained the remaining heads of department and superior *employés*. Each of these was to draw $\frac{1}{500}$th of the divisible sum for every thousand francs received in annual salary.

Under the third class came all other *employés* in the receipt of yearly salaries. They were jointly entitled to what remained of the distributable amount after the claims of the two preceding classes had been satisfied.

The sums assigned to members of the first class were to be paid over in immediate cash.

The annual share of each member of the second class was to be divided into two equal parts: one paid over to him in a ready money bonus, the other compulsorily invested for his benefit in a State security, and not withdrawable or assignable without the consent of the Company.

The individual distribution of the sum falling to the great mass of *employés* constituting the third class was provided for as follows. One-half was to go in rewards for distinguished service, and the other half to be divided among all the members of the class in proportion to their respective annual salaries. The rewards were to be handed over in cash, and the percentages on salaries to be compulsorily invested as in the case of members of the second class.

This method of distribution, applied in 1845 and 1846, was found to yield for members of the third class too small a share. Accordingly the following system was, in 1847, devised and substituted for it. The salaries coming under each class having been lumped, the total for the first class was multiplied by 3, that for the second by 2, that for the third by 1. The shares falling to the three classes were determined by dividing the whole distributable amount into three parts proportional to the above three products respectively. Individual distribution within each class took place in proportion to salaries received. This system, applied to the results of the year 1846, gave for the first class 56·6 per cent., for the second 37·8 per cent., and for the third 18·9 per cent. on the annual salaries received.

The Revolution of 1848 compelled a further change of system. A decree of the Minister of Public Works enacted that thenceforward amount of salary received should be the sole element employed to determine each individual's rate of participation.

The division of *employés* into classes for the purpose of assessing shares in profits necessarily at once ceased. In October, 1848, the question of abandoning the principle of participation was raised on the Board of Directors, but they decided to retain it.

The regulation of 1845, amended in 1847, was again revised and corrected in 1850. A clause was introduced abolishing the system of classing the *employés*, and enacting that their shares in profits should be uniformly distributed by handing over one-third in cash, investing one-third in the Savings Bank, and paying the remaining one-third into the State Pension Office (at that time projected) or into some other insurance office, for the purpose of constituting for each *employé* a life annuity of at least £24 to begin at the age of fifty.

In 1852 three other Railway Companies—those of the "Centre," of Bordeaux and of Nantes—were united with and absorbed in that of Orleans. It was expressly stipulated that the *employés* in the service of these three Companies should thenceforward "enjoy the same advantages of participation in profits as the *employés* of the Orleans Company."

After this fusion profits accrued so abundantly that the fixed charge of fifteen per cent. upon them brought the share of each *employé* to a very high figure—thirty-four per cent. on wages in 1852, and forty-one in 1853. At the general meeting on the 15th of November of the latter year, it was pointed out that these results were not in proportion to those on which participation had originally been calculated, and that there was need of modifying the statutes on this point.

The question having been examined, the general

meeting adopted a statutory modification by which the fixed charge of fifteen per cent. for the benefit of the *employés* was replaced by the following arrangement. After eight per cent. had been paid on share capital, fifteen per cent. on the remaining net profits were assigned to labour, provided the year's operations did not yield to the shareholders a total dividend greater than fifteen per cent. on their capital. If this percentage were overpassed, labour was to receive only ten per cent. on the profits exceeding the amount thus defined. Similarly when the year's yield gave a greater dividend than sixteen per cent. on capital, labour's share of the excess above the sum necessary to do this was reduced to five per cent.

On the 30th of March, 1854, a regulation was adopted that, in each year, a preferential charge not exceeding ten per cent. should be made on the sum allotted to the *employés*, and paid to a fund for providing aid in cases of accident, injury or infirmity, help to widows and prizes for distinguished services. This charge was also not to exceed that necessary to make up, with the balance of the previous year, a maximum of £10,000. This deduction having been effected, the remaining sum was to be allotted in proportion to wages or salaries and paid one-third in cash, one-third to the Paris Savings Bank, and one-third to the State Pension Office.

The above regulation made, as will have been noticed, no essential change in that of 1850. In 1863, however, a fresh regulation appeared which allowed the Benefit Fund to levy as much as fifteen per cent. on the sum available for participation, and altered the principle on which that sum had previously been disposed of. Allotment in proportion to pay received was retained, but division into three equal parts consisting respectively in cash, investment and pension-premium, gave place to the following arrangement.

The share in profits of each beneficiary was in the first place to be employed, *up to ten per cent. on his yearly wage-earnings*, in making annual payments on his behalf to the State Pension Office. Available surplus, *up to a further seven per cent. on the same sum*, was to be handed to him in ready money, and the residue, if any, paid to his Savings Bank account.

The following table * shows the number of participating *employés*, and the ratio borne by their shares in profits to their annual wages, for each year from the commencement of Profit-Sharing in 1844 down to 1882. The wages paid are fully on a level with those obtainable from non-participating French railway companies:—

Year.	No. of Participants.	Ratio of Share in Profits to Annual Wages.
1844	719	6·81 per cent.
1845	816	16·66 ,,
1846	957	25·53 ,,
1847	1269	22·21 ,,
1848	1305	1·72 ,,
1849	1065	17·73 ,,
1850	1025	14·28 ,,
1851	1084	22·33 ,,
1852	2800	34·11 ,,
1853	3365	40·96 ,,
1854	4397	25·00 ,,
1855	4837	27·00 ,,
1856	5187	24·00 ,,

* Kindly supplied to me by the Managing Director of the Company.

IV.] PARIS AND ORLEANS RAILWAY COMPANY. 83

Year.	No. of Participants.	Ratio of Share in Profits to Annual Wages.
1857	5,765	25·30 per cent.
1858	5,940	23·10 ,,
1859	6,009	23·75 ,,
1860	5,991	24·10 ,,
1861	6,052	23·50 ,,
1862	6,194	22·70 ,,
1863	6,742	21·60 ,,
1864	6,997	20·67 ,,
1865	9,712	14·40 ,,
1866	10,181	13·88 ,,
1867	10,472	13·23 ,,
1868	11,376	12·15 ,,
1869	12,220	10·98 ,,
1870	12,484	10·00 ,,
1871	12,890	12·15 ,,
1872	13,727	11·00 ,,
1873	14,165	10·60 ,,
1874	14,234	10·25 ,,
1875	14,481	10·20 ,,
1876	15,080	9·76 ,,
1877	15,293	9·40 ,,
1878	15,321	9·32 ,,
1879	15,423	9·26 ,,
1880	15,743	9·05 ,,
1881	16,085	10·00 ,,
1882	16,935	10·00 ,,

The entire sum allotted out of profits to the *employés* for the above period is £2,583,378.

Reference to the preceding table will show that from 1864 onwards the ratio of the *employés*' share in profits to their wages steadily declined until, in 1870, it only just reached ten per cent. As the regulation of 1863 permitted no distribution in ready money until this percentage on wages had been paid to the Pension Office, the *cash* dividend to labour necessarily dwindled from 4·4 per cent. in 1865 to *nil* in 1870. The effect of this disappearance of bonus, and of a too restricted application of the Benefit Fund, was thus described by M. Charles Robert * before the Paris Social Economy Society on the 1st of May, 1870:—

Participation, doubtless not from fault in the principle, but in consequence of certain administrative proceedings, no longer bears in the Orleans Company the fruits which it produced ten years ago, in 1860 for instance. The spur has become somewhat blunted. Formerly participation procured for those entitled to it two simultaneous advantages, a yearly bonus and a right to pension. The addition of less productive lines of railway has diminished the distributable amount. Further, the regulation permitting variable sums to be granted to *employés* for distinguished service is worked in such a manner that for the mass of subordinates participation in profits no longer produces either bonus or reward. It is solely equivalent to an eventual right to pension and the *employés* of the Orleans Company henceforth much resemble those of the State Offices.

Applied as, for instance, it was in 1858, participation exercised on the staff of the Orleans Company a considerable influence. The deep and living feeling of a real and serious identity of interests gave to this *personnel* the appearance of a vast family. The *employés* mutually looked after each other. They had constantly in mind the thought of an eventual profit to be shared, of a possible loss to be avoided. Thus every one showed the greatest care in handling the passengers' luggage, and if an *employé* treated it unceremoniously a comrade was not unfrequently heard saying to him, "What are you about? You will shorten our dividend!" I have these details from a witness of authority. . . . But the cash dividend to the staff of the Orleans Company having come to nothing, the zeal and emulation of a good number among them have disappeared together with the hope of this legitimate remuneration. *Cessante causâ, cessat effectus.*

The history of Profit-Sharing in the Orleans Company falls into three periods.

* President of the French Participation Society.

The first, which extends from 1843 to 1848, shows a genuine ready-money participation, constituted by a charge of so much per cent. on the receipts distributed at variable rates corresponding to the different classes of *employés* who form the *personnel* of a great company. A very important share was assigned to the executive body, heads of department and superior *employés*.

The second period begins with the Revolution of 1848. Ideas of equality having got the upper hand, the differing rates for different classes of *employés* disappear, and Profit-Sharing among them all takes place in a uniform manner proportionately to wages or salary. The sum allotted to each is now divided into three equal parts: the first is handed over in cash; the second is credited to a Savings Bank account withdrawable only with the consent of the Board of Directors; the third is paid to the State Pension Office. During this period the share in profits reaches, in 1853, nearly forty-one per cent. on each *employé's* earnings.

The third period, the starting-point of which is marked by the application of the regulation of 1863, and by a diminution of profits, begins with the year 1865. The regulation orders that the share in profits be first applied, up to ten per cent. on wages received, to a payment to the Pension Office. This share is in process of diminution, and there will soon, under the operation of the new regulation, be hardly anything left to be distributed in ready money or put into the Savings Bank. In fact, on the one side the fusion of other lines of railway with that of Orleans has involved a considerable increase of *personnel* without a proportionate increase of receipts, and on the other the Company finds itself compelled to appeal to the State guarantee. While this guarantee remains in force, and until the complete reimbursement to be made to the State of all sums advanced by it on this score, the allotment to the *employés* of a sum equal to ten per cent. on their annual earnings has been allowed to rank among the working expenses, and the State makes up this percentage in virtue of its guarantee. This participation by the *employés*, or rather the subvention which supplements it, is thus maintained in spite of losses which the Company may incur. For a lacking profit is substituted a charge under general expenses. This charge has for its sole object to ensure the regular payment to the Pension Office of the ten per cent. on wages entitling to annuities the inadequacy of which is now engaging the serious attention of the Orleans Company, though in such a position of affairs a cash bonus is of course out of the question. The articles of the Statutes and Regulations relative to participation still remain, but if participation itself continues to exist, it is in a latent state. Its animation is suspended so long as the State guarantee continues to operate.

ESSAY V.

PROFIT-SHARING IN AGRICULTURE.

(*Nineteenth Century*, October, 1882.)

IN preceding Essays I have described the beneficial results accruing, both to employers and employed, from the system of remuneration which allots to labour, in addition to fixed wages, a share in the profits realised. The material success attainable by the application of this system to a given branch of industry depends on the extent to which the operatives engaged in it are able, by supplying more efficient work, to enhance the profits of enterprise. This influence of labour upon profits can be exerted in three ways : by increasing the quantity, improving the quality and diminishing the cost of production. In forecasting the result likely to ensue from the introduction of profit-sharing into an assigned undertaking we have, therefore, only to estimate the degree in which the stimulated zeal of the men employed will bring about the three effects just enumerated.

From this point of view, agriculture would seem to offer an exceptionally promising field for the system under consideration. The slack, clumsy and wasteful character of the work done by agricultural labourers under existing arrangements is a matter of general complaint. Could these shortcomings be converted into the opposite excellences, there can be no doubt that an abundant source of fresh profit would at once be opened. As, however, purely theoretical considerations have but little weight with men engaged in practical business, it is fortunate that, in the present instance, an appeal can be made to the results of actual experiments in participatory farming successfully carried out on the Continent.

In the now depressed condition of our agriculture, when every expedient which seems to offer a prospect of improved production is anxiously canvassed, no apology is needed for the attempt here made to place on record the salient features of a few conspicuous applications of profit-sharing to that all-important industry. The facts to be alleged are, with but few exceptions, taken from Böhmert's great work * the statements of which may be accepted with entire confidence as they were obtained by direct correspondence with the agriculturists by whom the experiments which he describes were instituted or carried on.

Among the instances selected, the post of honour is due to the organisation which has been at work from 1847 to the present time on the estate Tellow,

* *Die Gewinnbetheiligung.* Leipzig, Brockhaus, 1878. In this work will be found full technical details on the cases selected for brief description in the present Essay, as well as on other instances of profit-sharing applied to agriculture. I have referred for more recent information to a paper by the same author, reprinted from the *Arbeiterfreund*, Berlin, Simion, 1880.

near Teterow, in Mecklenburg-Schwerin. Herr J. H. von Thünen, proprietor of that estate at the date referred to, who is remembered in Germany as a writer of repute on economical questions, commenced his experiment on the following plan. To all his regularly employed workpeople occupying cottages on the estate he assigned, over and above ordinary wages paid at the full rate current in the neighbourhood, a share in the profits of farming. At the close of each year's account, on the 30th of June, an inventory was to be made, and the value of everything on hand estimated. Increase in value over the preceding year was to be reckoned as additional receipt; diminution set down as loss.

If, after deduction of all outgoings, the profits exceeded £825, each participant was to have one-half per cent. of the surplus above this amount. When, on the contrary, the assigned limit was not attained, the deficit was to be made good out of the next year's surplus. The number of beneficiaries, including bailiff, schoolmaster, cartwright, etc., was twenty-one.

The individual share in profits was not paid in cash, but credited to a savings account. On the sum therein standing Herr von Thünen paid $4\frac{1}{8}$* per cent. interest, which was handed over each year in the form of a cash bonus at Christmas. Only at sixty years of age could a participant draw the capital sum accumulated for him. Should he die sooner, it passed to his widow, subject in some cases to partial settlement upon children.

The above arrangement is still in force, with no

* The interest paid now is four per cent.

important change save that the sum above which participation begins is now £900 instead of £825. Herr von Thünen's son, and his grandson Herr A. von Thünen the present proprietor, both had full power to abolish the system, but they preferred to retain it.

The following table shows the sum annually allotted to each participant, for himself and his family, since the introduction of the system:—

	£	s.	d.		£	s.	d.
1847-48	1	12	0	1865-66	0	6	0
1848-49	1	9	0	1866-67	1	10	0
1849-50	2	17	0	1867-68	4	5	0
1850-51	3	4	0	1868-69	4	0	0
1851-52	2	2	0	1869-70	3	14	0
1852-53	1	14	0	1870-71	4	1	0
1853-54	3	11	0	1871-72	4	10	0
1854-55	6	17	0	1872-73	4	1	0
1855-56	4	3	0	1873-74	2	0	0
1856-57	5	3	0	1874-75	4	10	0
1857-58	4	6	0	1875-76	0	17	0
1858-59	4	7	0	1876-77		—	
1859-60	4	7	0	1877-78	0	19	6
1860-61	4	12	0	1878-79	0	13	0
1861-62	1	13	0	1879-80	2	10	0
1862-63	7	12	0	1880-81	4	8	0
1863-64	7	16	0	1881-82	3	18	0
1864-65	4	17	0				

In the unfavourable year 1876-77 there was a deficit of £439 below the stipulated minimum of £900. This was made good out of the surpluses of the two succeeding years. Herr A. von Thünen expressed the following opinion of the general results of the system followed at Tellow, in a letter to Professor Böhmert dated the 25th of May, 1877:—

The institution has approved itself and borne the fruits which my grandfather hoped from it, at least with the majority of our people: exceptions are, of course, to be met with here as everywhere. The share in profits retains the people on the estate, as, if they quit it, they do not receive their capital, but only the interest upon it. It creates common aims for the proprietor and the labourers, and so, brings about a better understanding between the two parties. At the outset most of the people were, I believe, somewhat dissatisfied because their share was not paid over in cash. But by slow degrees, as the capital of individuals grew, they recognised the excellence of the system on this point also, for with many of them the interest which they receive in an ordinary year exceeds the share of profits annually allotted to them.

In a letter addressed to me on the 2nd of November, 1881, Herr A. von Thünen expressed a continued favourable opinion of the system in action at Tellow. "The results of the participatory arrangement here are," he wrote, "very gratifying."

An experiment carried on from 1872 to 1877 at Bredow in the neighbourhood of Berlin, by Herr H. Jahnke, on a farm partly freehold and partly leasehold, presents features of much interest. In consequence of the dearness, scarcity and inefficiency of the work obtainable from hired labourers in his district, Herr Jahnke entered, in January, 1872, upon the following arrangement with five married labourers. He and they were to form an association for cultivating his farm to the best advantage; Herr Jahnke undertaking to provide stock and capital, and to pay rent, taxes and all other outgoings. For his own services in directing the farming operations and keeping the accounts he was to draw a salary of £45 as a first charge on profits. Each associated labourer was to have a good cottage and a piece of garden land rent free, besides allowances in turf, wood, etc. The five men together were to receive 52*s.* 6*d.* as weekly wages in summer, and 45*s.* in winter. The proprietor was to credit to himself an amount equal to the whole sum thus annually paid to the labourers. Of the net profits accruing in each year one half was to belong to Herr Jahnke, and the other half to be divided among the associated labourers The five men agreed to do, with some help from their wives and children, the whole work of the farm, and, if occasional extra labour proved requisite, to supply this at their own cost. They further undertook to deposit 30*s.* each as caution-money, and to invest in their employer's custody not less than 30*s.* out of each annual share in profits accruing to them. On this caution-money and on their subsequent investments Herr Jahnke was to pay interest at five per cent. An agreement to the above effect was made for five years from April, 1872.

The material results of the experiment are given by Böhmert for only the first three years of its continuance. They were as follows :—

Year.	Total Net Profits.	Employer's Share.	Each Labourer's entire Earnings in Wages and Share of Profits.
	£ *s.* *d.*	£ *s.* *d.*	£ *s.* *d.*
1872–73	527 19 6	263 19 9	52 16 0
1873–74	488 8 5	244 4 3	48 16 10
1874–75	549 6 6	274 13 3	54 18 8

Each associated labourer, therefore, received on an average £52 3*s.* in money during each of these three years. If to this be added, as Herr Jahnke thinks should be done, £61 5s. as the equivalent of house and garden rent, and of allowances in turf, wood, potatoes, butter, etc., there results a total of £58 18s. 10d.

Professor von der Goltz, in a work published in 1875, estimated the highest annual earnings of agricultural labourers in the German Empire at £33 4s. Even though this estimate be, as seems probable, somewhat below the truth, the contrast to the advantage of Herr Jahnke's system remains, from the labourer's point of view, very marked.

As a measure of the material benefits conferred on the employer may be taken Herr Jahnke's statement that his land, which he would have been willing to sell in 1872 for £4500, might, he thought, have fetched £5100 if it had been offered for sale in 1875, by which time ten per cent. more ground had been brought under the plough by the exertions of his labourers.

Herr Jahnke's principal objects in the introduction of profit-sharing were to ensure a constant supply of zealous labourers and avoid fluctuations in wages, to encourage thrift and to increase agricultural production. He considered his system to have been *thoroughly successful* in attaining these objects.

No details later than 1875 are given on Herr Jahnke's authority. It appears, however, that two of his labourers subsequently quitted his employment in order to set up on their own account. In 1877 he sold his property, and the participatory arrangement at once came to an end, as the purchaser could not make up his mind to continue it. The cause which led to this result was one scarcely to have been anticipated—the hostility of the neighbouring proprietors to the profit-sharing system. "I must admit," wrote Herr Jahnke in 1877, "that by introducing this arrangement I made myself many enemies among the landed proprietors, and that it was this circumstance which induced me to part with the estate." He had already in 1875 described the opponents of participation as comprising proprietors who were for high prices and low wages, labourers who wanted high wages for a small quantity of bad work and such persons as found their advantage in the misunderstanding existing between agricultural employers and employed.

Böhmert appends to his account of the above experiment extracts from a paper by Herr Berthold Wölbling, a few passages of which I translate here.

After remarking on the increased earnings of labour under the half-profit system, Wölbling writes:—

> These earnings have a special source of their own, viz. enhanced production due to the industry and care of the labourers. Every practical farmer knows how imperfectly agricultural work is done by hirelings of all sorts, and how little what goes by the name of good superintendence is able actually to effect in securing good execution of work. The full effect of any work is brought about, not merely by intensified exertion of muscular force, but also by zeal and alertness of mind: such an application of bodily and mental powers is only to be obtained from one *whose entire interests are engaged*. In fact new springs of production are thus opened, and it is this which gives to the system its high agricultural importance. The labourer finds that his increased incomings are, relatively speaking, more easily earned than under fixed wages, because they include payment for carefulness as well as for mere efforts of brute force. A reciprocal influence on the habits of the labourers will also not fail to show itself. If they perceive that a successful result depends not merely on muscular exertion, but also on sustained orderliness and attention, they

will find it more and more their interest to practise these virtues.

The proprietor derives, independently of the pecuniary result, many advantages from the half-profit system. He has perfectly trustworthy labourers, and each piece of work is taken in hand at the proper moment. He is no longer obliged to urge and drive, while fretting internally at the many instances of neglect which he is powerless to prevent. When his back is turned, he knows that his business is as well attended to as if he were directing it himself. He can dispense with all intermediaries, as no formal overseeing is required. Nevertheless, the position of the managing head has grown in importance. He must show more than was formerly necessary that his management is sound, and that with regard to every department of his business he is firm in the saddle, for he now has a responsibility towards his associated labourers. He is more than ever bound to set them an example of diligence, economy and other virtues, on the exercise of which the success of the whole undertaking depends. In short, the system demands a thoroughly competent man.

Baron Zytphen-Adeler, member of the "Landsthings" or First Chamber of the Danish Parliament, commenced in 1873, on his estate named Dragsholm, Zealand, Denmark, a very important experiment in the application of profit-sharing to agriculture. He gave notice that for the year 1873-74 all net profits exceeding a specified amount should, with the exception of a small sum (£22 10s.) reserved to be distributed as prizes for specially good conduct, be divided into two equal parts, one of which would go to the proprietor, and the other be divided among all the persons—over eighty in number—employed in cultivating his estate. A detailed schedule assigned the proportions in which each was to participate, according to the importance of the duties which he discharged. Thus the chief dairyman was to have ten per cent., the housekeeper five per cent., and each day-labourer one per cent. of the distributable bonus. One-fourth of the share allotted to each individual was to be compulsorily invested in a savings account, the remainder to be paid over on the spot. These shares in profits were of course independent of and additional to ordinary market wages.

For the year 1873-74 the divisible bonus amounted to £236. In distributing it the number of days which each labourer had worked was taken into account. The maximum obtained by a field-hand was £2 11s. 6d.; the average about £1. When announcing these results, Baron Zytphen-Adeler carefully explained to his workpeople the essential conditions of participatory success.

The next year, 1874-75, was marked by an extremely unfavourable rape-harvest, the yield being but little over one-third of that in the previous year. Heavier outlay and an increased rate of wages had also to be met. The share assigned to labour sank to £170, but the effect of the system in evoking improved work was plainly visible. "I have," said the proprietor in a report on the agricultural year, "been able to observe distinctly a fuller recognition of this fact, that it is the interest of every man to devote himself to his work with industry and conscientiousness."

Only in the third year of the experiment did the good results of the system fully manifest themselves. Baron Zytphen-Adeler expressed his firm conviction that its principles were now really understood by his workpeople. In proof of this he alleged the fact that on his estate—the largest agricultural undertaking in Zealand—the entire harvest had been got in a week earlier than on many small holdings. This had never been done before, and the result was achieved only by the sustained zeal of all concerned. After remarking that the significance of this fact would escape no agriculturist, the Baron added the following corroborative incident:—"One day rye was being sown: when, at half-past seven in the evening, I found the people still hard at work, I remarked that they would anyhow not succeed in finishing on that day the two acres and a half still remaining to be sown. They, however, answered with one voice that *that must* be done; and it *was* done!"

The sum available for the year 1875–76 as bonus to labour was £313. One field-hand with his wife and children received, exclusively of prizes for good conduct, nearly £7, a second £6, a third £5, and so on.

The year 1876–77 produced, in consequence of a bad harvest, a result so unsatisfactory that not even the preliminary minimum assigned to the proprietor could be covered, and that a bonus to the labourers was entirely out of the question. It was carefully explained to them that the bad harvest rendered any other result impossible. No sign of discontent showed itself—a clear indication that they had fully recognised the inevitable vicissitudes to which agricultural production is subject.

The above are the latest details of this experiment with which I am acquainted.

My object in placing before the reader in rough outline a few specimens of profit-sharing successfully applied to Continental agriculture is to bespeak practical attention for the question under what form that system may, with the best chances of success, be introduced into British farming. To elaborate a plan of organisation is obviously a task to which no one but a practical agriculturist is competent; and even he would probably hold that, in applying the system to any particular case, the individual circumstances of that case must be carefully considered and provided for. Without usurping however the functions of the agricultural specialist, I may, in terminating this Essay, refer briefly to one or two points which cannot be safely neglected in any application of the system.

In order to guard the interests of the employer, a sum should be determined upon and notified as representing the minimum return on his capital, and remuneration for his own services, which will satisfy him. Only the surplus profits above this sum should constitute the participation-fund; and therefore, when this sum was not overpassed, no bonus should be allotted to labour.

As, however, the success of the system wholly depends on the degree in which the prospect held out to the labourers leads them to contribute improved work, the limit just mentioned ought to be put at the lowest point consistent with reasonable safety to the employer's capital. The proportion, too, of the surplus profits assigned to labour ought to be fixed at an attractive figure. Any scheme to which either too high a minimum, or too low a rate of bonus, gave the look of having been constructed in order to enable the employer to pocket the result of his labourers' additional exertions, would be foredoomed to failure.

A doubt may be felt as to how far so uneducated a class as English agricultural labourers unfortunately still are can be made to understand the central principle of profit-sharing, and so be induced to put forth the sustained efforts necessary to reap its fruits. The experience gained during the short-lived participatory experiment made half a century ago in Ireland seems, however, eminently fitted to remove such hesitation. That, during a crisis of agrarian violence far exceeding in intensity anything recently enacted in that country, the labourers on Mr. Vandeleur's estate at Ralahine, county Clare, were induced by the influence of participation to work with extraordinary energy and remarkable success, is a notorious fact.* A principle sufficiently luminous to have been clearly recognised by this group of disaffected men, some of whom had just before assisted in or connived at the treacherous murder of their own steward, can surely be made adequately comprehensible to the present generation of British labourers.

* See Appendix to this Essay.

APPENDIX TO ESSAY V.

[I place here an extract from a Paper read by me at the Dublin Meeting of the Social Science Association, 1881, on the question "What results may be expected to arise from an Extension of the System of Participation by Labour in the Profits of Manufacturing, Agricultural and Trading Enterprises?"]

To agricultural production has been assigned in the question before us a distinctive position merited, not only by its paramount importance to the people of Ireland, but also, as I believe, by the specially promising field which it offers for participatory operations. I propose, therefore, to treat this branch of our subject in some detail.

It will be remembered that two conditions are essential to successful profit-sharing. The zeal of the workers must be adequately enlisted, and labour must be able to exert an effective influence on production. That in British agriculture the second condition is satisfied—that more active and intelligent efforts on the part of the labourers would lead to improved returns—admits of no doubt. The only question to be answered is therefore this:—Can agricultural labourers be induced, by the prospect which participation offers, to put forth the sustained exertions necessary to secure its benefits? It would be easy to produce affirmative replies to this question from Continental authorities. . . . Under present restrictions of time, however, I shall only appeal to a single remarkably instructive experiment made half a century ago in Ireland during a social crisis far more severe than that which has visited it during the present year.

The time was one of acute agrarian suffering, discontent and violence. "The peasantry," says the *Annual Register* for 1831, " marched in bands through the counties, demanding reduction of rents and increase of wages, and threatening destruction to the magistrates and gentry who should disobey or endeavour to resist. . . . In some instances they insisted that no mode of agriculture should be used but that which should employ the greatest number of hands, such as spade husbandry. In the county of Meath, they marched from house to house, taking the labourers from their work and the horses from the plough : and as soon as the military had dispersed one assemblage at one point, a new one started up at another.*

". . . In the counties of Clare, Roscommon, Galway and Tipperary the law seemed no longer to exist. Murder, robbery, searching for arms—these things done, too, by bodies of men who could be met only by military force—were the ordinary occurrences of every day. . . . In the county of Clare, in particular, all decent persons of all opinions affirmed that the country was no longer tolerable as a place of residence. The serving of threatening notices, the levelling of walls, the driving off of cattle, the beating of herdsmen, the compulsory removal of tenants, the levying of contributions in money, the robbery of dwelling-houses, the reckless commission of murder, were driving the better class of inhabitants to desert their houses and seek refuge in some other quarter." † Such were the

* Page 302. † Ibid., pp. 324, 325.

conditions under which Mr. John Scott Vandeleur, a landed proprietor in the county of Clare, had the courage to undertake an experiment in participatory agriculture. The scene of it was an estate of 618 acres called "Ralahine," situated between Limerick and Ennis, and surrounding Mr. Vandeleur's dwelling-house. The experiment and its results are fully described in Pare's *Co-operative Agriculture*,* a work the materials for which were mainly, I understand, supplied by Mr. E. T. Craig, who was the secretary, and to a considerable extent the practical organiser, of the Ralahine Association. The following account of the experiment is condensed from the narrative given by Pare.

Mr. Vandeleur had, since 1823, been a disciple and friend of Robert Owen. Finding himself embarrassed in the cultivation of Ralahine by the ignorance and drunkenness of his labourers, and by their intense aversion to be directed in their work by a steward, he determined to give participation a trial, nor was he deterred from, but rather confirmed in, his purpose by the treacherous murder of his own steward, perpetrated not long before the commencement of the experiment and with at least the connivance of some of his own labourers. The agreement, made in November, 1831, between the proprietor and the whole body of workpeople, men, women and children, fifty-two in all, on the Ralahine estate, was as follows. Mr. Vandeleur was to supply the land, buildings, implements, stock and stores, and to pay daily wages at the ordinary rate. The "Association," of which

* Longmans, 1870.

the workpeople were constituted members, Mr. Vandeleur president, and Mr. Craig secretary, was to supply to the proprietor produce to the estimated value of £900 as rent for his land and interest on his capital. The net profits were to belong to the Association, but were to be expended, not in individual distribution, but in purchasing the live stock from Mr. Vandeleur, and for other objects advantageous to the Association as a body.

The experiment while it lasted was successful beyond all expectation, but unfortunately, before two years had elapsed from the signature of the original agreement, a single act of deplorable weakness totally unconnected with the proceedings of the Association put an immediate and calamitous end to the entire undertaking. Mr. Vandeleur, though a high-minded and benevolent man, was disastrously addicted to gambling. At his club in Dublin he indulged this passion to the extent of sacrificing to it everything he possessed in the world. His total ruin fell on the little community at Ralahine with the effect of an avalanche. A *fiat* in bankruptcy was taken out against his estate, and, as the Association had no lease and their "agreement" was legally invalid, they were summarily ejected without any compensation, and the land was seized for the benefit of the creditors.

Short-lived as was the Ralahine experiment, it has put on record invaluable experience as to the results of participatory agriculture on those brought under its influence. A few quotations from Mr. Pare's book will indicate of what kind these results were.

The first extract shows the capacity of participation to elicit increased zeal in work.

"We formerly," said one of the labourers in speaking of their condition when working under the direction of a steward, "had no interest either in doing a great deal of work, doing it well, or in suggesting improvements, as all the advantages and all the praise were given to a tyrannical taskmaster for his attention and watchfulness. We were looked upon as merely machines, and his business was to keep us in motion; for this reason it took the time of three or four of us to watch him, and, when he was fairly out of sight, you may depend we did not hurt ourselves by too much labour; but now that our interest and our duty are made to be the same, we have no need of a steward at all." *

"At harvest-time," said Mr. Craig, "the whole Society used voluntarily to work longer than the time specified,† and I have seen the whole body occasionally, at these seasons, act with such energy and accomplish such great results by their united exertions, that each and all seemed as if fired by a wild enthusiastic determination to achieve some glorious enterprise—and that, too, without any additional stimulant being administered to them in the shape of extra pecuniary reward." ‡

The next quotation illustrates the carefulness in the preservation of property which participation calls forth.

"It is proverbial that an Irishman is ever ripe for

---

* Pare, pp. 60, 61.
† Compare the testimony of Baron Zytphen-Adeler, *ante*, p. 97.
‡ Pare, p. 62.

excitement. Its kind and force will very much depend upon circumstances. He will either carry you on his back or lay you on your own, as you may treat him. During the hunting season it was customary with many of the peasantry to join in the chase for some distance, when the fox took across lands near where they were at their labour. In doing this they would pass over and trample down the young crops, and break down the fences, with as much *nonchalance* as the most legitimate huntsman who ever followed hounds—from whom, indeed, the lesson had been learned. A good run over the fields in chase of Reynard was held as capital fun.

"When, however, the members of the Association began to realise their true position, they would not permit any one to disturb the fences, or to hunt over the estate. During the winter of 1832, a hunted fox crossed the mill water-course near the rick-yard, and took across the orchard, and over a seventy-acre field of wheat in the highest tilth of any land on the estate. The mounted huntsmen—young squires, farmers and tradesmen—to keep well up with the hounds on the wheat-field would have to pass through the farm-yard, but they found that, by a sudden and mutual impulse, the large high gates of the farm-yard had been locked against them by the 'New Systemites.' Many of the huntsmen seemed perfectly astounded at the daring and 'impudence' of these men. The incident shows that the new system had converted these once indifferent or careless servants into prudent conservators of the property under their care."*

* Pare, pp. 117, 118.

"Before the Society was established," said Mr. Craig, "the labourers conceived their own interest opposed to that of their employers, and would attend to nothing beyond their appointments for the passing moment. If a bullock broke over a fence and trampled down the wheat, they would say, 'It's no business of ours; let the herdsmen see to it;' and thus the wheat was destroyed because they got neither profit nor thanks for their extra trouble. They conceived it to be their interest to encourage clandestinely the destruction of property, believing that it would create a greater demand for their labour. But after the Society commenced this order of things was reversed. A single potato was by many of them very reluctantly wasted, for they found that the conservation of the property was the saving of their own labour. Thus the same faculty of mind—self-interest—produced opposite results when surrounded by opposite controlling circumstances." *

A few months before the final catastrophe Mr. Vandeleur described the results to be anticipated from a wide extension of the system in the following words, part of an address to his labourers on the employment of machinery in agriculture :—

"Tell the owners of land that, if they wish to use machinery beneficially, they should form you into societies where it cannot injure you, but where you would have an interest in using and protecting it. And should they be induced to unite with you in these arrangements so advantageous to all parties, they would soon see a great, wonderful, and rapid improve-

* Pare, p. 118.

ment in the state of the country; there would be no more *starvation in the midst of abundance*, nor any necessity for industrious workmen to leave their homes, friends and country, for foreign woods and wilds, whilst their native land remains but partially cultivated." *

The verdict of the Ralahine labourers as to the effect of the experiment on themselves is contained in the following statement agreed to at the last general meeting of the Association:—" We the undersigned have experienced for the last two years contentment, peace and happiness under the arrangements introduced by Mr. Vandeleur and Mr. E. T. Craig. At the commencement we were opposed to the plans proposed by them; but, on their introduction, we found our condition improved, our wants more regularly attended to, and our feelings towards each other at once entirely changed from jealousy, hatred, and revenge, to confidence, friendship, and forbearance." †

The eminently encouraging results attained at Ralahine under eminently discouraging circumstances seem to constitute a strong argument in favour of renewed experiments of the same, or of a kindred, description. The requisites are land, capital and labour. We hear of farms unlet, of capital pent up in banks for lack of safe investments, and, in parts of Ireland at any rate, of a redundant agricultural population. On the other hand, the evil to which Mr. Vandeleur pointed, "starvation in the midst of abundance," is still uneradicated, and emigration is

* Pare, pp. 69, 70.   † Ibid., pp. 137, 138.

far from being a completely satisfactory cure. Can there, then, be a doubt that, with need so urgent and conditions so favourable, the remedy for agricultural weakness which participation seems to offer ought, with no further delay, to be submitted to conclusive trials made upon an adequate scale?

ESSAY VI.

PROFIT-SHARING IN DISTRIBUTIVE ENTERPRISE.

(Part of a Paper read on the 15th of October, 1881, before the Southern Section of the Co-operative Board.)

[After a brief introduction on the beneficial results attained by profit-sharing in productive industry, the paper continued as follows :—]

Such, sketched in the barest outline, are the salient results of profit-sharing. It would be easy both to enlarge the picture and to fill in details to an almost unlimited extent. I am, however, anxious to pass from general considerations on the subject before us, to its application in a particular branch of industry with which the members of this Conference are closely connected,—I mean distributive trading. The managing committee of a Co-operative Store—and many such committees are represented by the delegates here assembled—occupies essentially the position of a distributive trader. This being so, the application of profit-sharing to distributive enterprise must necessarily possess a priority of interest in the minds of those present. I shall, therefore, on this occasion pass over the immensely important organisations of the system in productive establishments, in order to describe, with such fulness as limited time will allow, a conspicuous distributive house working on a participatory basis in the French capital.

The "*Magasin du Bon Marché*," rue du Bac, and adjoining streets, Paris, is a huge establishment for the sale of all kinds of manufactured goods, which employs some three thousand persons, superior officials, clerks, salesmen and saleswomen, and attendants of various grades. The founder and builder of this vast undertaking was M. Jacques Aristide Boucicaut, whose character well bore out a Christian name embodying the old Greek standard of what a "just man" ought to be. A few words on M. Boucicaut's career are indispensable in order to bring out clearly the object of the institution which he created. I translate the following short account of his life from the *Bulletin** of the French Participation Society, from which also the rest of this paper has been compiled :—

M. Jacques Aristide Boucicaut was born in 1809 at Bellême (Orne). The son of a hatter in a small way of business, he had to begin early his apprenticeship to a laborious life. The retail trade in stuffs used formerly to be carried on in the country by salesmen travelling from town to town, and it was in this way that the young Boucicaut began his career. He accompanied one of these perambulating vendors in a very subordinate capacity; while the goods were being unpacked at the inns, he had to look after the horses and van. His situation was precarious and often unhappy.

Before long he came to Paris and entered as *employé* the *Magasins du Petit Saint Thomas* where he rapidly distinguished

---

* 1883, pp. 3, 4.

himself, and became superintendent and purchaser. Thanks to great personal efforts, he succeeded in educating himself: he loved books and was naturally inclined to study. His duty taking him several times to England, he managed, by dint of energy and patience, to learn English, constantly studying in the coach or in the railway carriage his grammar or his reading-book. It was in 1852 that he acquired the establishment, then a very modest one, called the "*Bon Marché*" to the development of which he applied all the powers of his high intelligence, prodigious activity, accurate taste, and commanding capacity of directing a vast organisation and at the same time keeping a firm grasp on the smallest and seemingly most insignificant details. Persons who knew M. Boucicaut say that to all these gifts were added a happily constituted character, excellence of heart and perfect uprightness.

From the day when he felt himself justified in counting on a durable success, he determined to put his philanthropic ideas into practice. He had set out from the lowest rung, he had painfully climbed all the successive steps of his business, he had seen other *employés* suffer, and suffered himself, from abuses inherent in the current modes of doing business: his desire was that the experience he had so laboriously gained should not be lost, but should one day prove of service to all engaged in his branch of trade.

His favourite idea, the thought nearest his heart, was to raise the condition, moral and material, of the persons in his own line of life; he had belonged to the class of commercial *employés* who used to be designated by the nickname "counter-jumpers;" he held it a point of honour to show what the young people who follow this career may be and ought to be, and especially to assist those whose capacities were not adequate for the attainment of the lucrative posts of head of department or superior *employé*.

M. Boucicaut's material success was extremely great. His establishment, when he acquired it in 1852, was doing a business of not more than £18,000 a-year; in 1869 the annual turn-over was £840,000— an increase of 4500 per cent. in seventeen years.

The year 1876 witnessed the introduction—which had been delayed by the disastrous events brought upon Paris in the train of the Franco-German War—of a long-meditated system of profit-sharing by which a direct interest in the prosperity of the *Maison Boucicaut* was thrown open to a large and constantly increasing number of its *employés*. A Provident Society was formed for their benefit, to be supported exclusively by sums annually paid over for that purpose out of the net profits of the house. A separate account was opened in the name of each member of this Society in order to be credited with his or her allotted share of each such successive payment. These annual dividends to labour were to accumulate at compound interest for an assigned number of years, and only at the expiration of that period was the resulting capital sum—save in exceptional cases—to be handed over to the person in whose name it stood.

The object for which this institution was created and the mode in which it was intended to work appear from the following words addressed by M. Boucicaut, in his own name and in that of his son, to the *employés* of the house when, on the 31st of July, 1876, he announced the establishment of the Provident Society:—

Our object has been to ensure to every one of our *employés* the possession of a small capital coming into his disposal at old age, or which, in case of death, may be a benefit to his family.

We wished at the same time to show them in an efficient way what is the close identity of aims which ought to unite them to the house.

They will better understand that their activity in work, attention to the interests of the house and economic treatment of the materials entrusted to them, are so many duties which turn to the profit of each and all.

They will be more thoroughly imbued with the principles which we never cease to set before them ; they will know the better, from being more directly interested, that success depends on their efforts, on their good conduct and on the care with which they endeavour to satisfy the customers—an object which we are one and all seeking to attain.

A few details, extracted from the printed regulations of the Provident Society, will show what were to be the qualification for membership and the terms of participation.

Every *employé* who had worked continuously for five years in the house had a right to membership— unless he happened to belong to the small class of superior officials who already possessed a direct interest in the sales effected in their several departments, or in the general business of the house. This arrangement obviously provided for a steady annual increase in the number of *employés* to whom the benefits of participation were to be extended.

Except in the opening year, for which a special arrangement was made, the sum annually paid over to the Society out of the profits of the house was to be allotted in the following manner :—

A separate account, opened in the name of each participant, was to be yearly credited with a share of this sum proportional to the amount which the *employé* in question had received in wages during the year on which the division was made.

Each such account was to be further credited in every successive year with interest at four per cent. on the whole amount standing in it. An annuity accumulating at compound interest for a term of years was thus assigned to each beneficiary.

The conditions under which the capital sums accumulated in this manner were to come into the actual disposal of the benefited persons were as follows:—

A male *employé*, either on attaining the age of sixty or on completing twenty years of uninterrupted work for the house, could claim cash payment of the entire sum standing to his credit. In the case of women the qualifying periods were to be fifty years of age or fifteen years of work.

While a long-deferred participation was thus created as the ordinary rule, exceptional cases were to be promptly provided for. On the death of a member of the Society, of whatever age or standing, immediate full payment to surviving relatives was statutably directed.

In the event of disabling illness recourse could be had, subject to approval by the heads of the firm, to partial or entire liquidation of account.

Such was M. Boucicaut's plan for securing to his *employés* an accumulated capital. The scale on which it was to be carried into effect, the actual amount to be in each or any year paid out of profits to the Provident Society, he reserved absolutely for his own unrestricted decision.

Unfortunately it was on but two occasions, in 1876 and 1877, that he was permitted to exercise this power. He died on the 26th of December in the latter year, and, ten months afterwards, death removed his son also. His widow succeeded alike to the ownership and direction of the house and to the maintenance of its organisation and traditions.

The sums yearly paid over to the Provident Society from its foundation in 1876 down to Midsummer, 1883, together with the number of its members in each of those years, were as follows :—

Year.	Sums paid to the Society.	No. of Members.
	£	
1876	2460	128
1877	2400	199
1878	3200	275
1879	3400	351
1880	3600	443
1881	3800	515
1882	4000	592
1883	4000	699

The property of the Society amounted on the 1st of August, 1883, to £26,453.

In January, 1880, the proprietress of the *Bon Marché*, as an act of respect to the memory of her husband, carried his ideas a step further by formally admitting into partnership with herself ninety-six heads of department and other *employés*, who put sums not less than £2000 each, and not more than £4000 each, into the business. In some instances these sums, though standing in a single name, were contributed by a group of *employés*, so that the benefits of partnership were actually extended to a larger number of persons than those named in the articles of association. The whole capital employed in the *Bon Marché* under the new arrangement is £800,000, of which Madame Boucicaut holds £500,000 and the partner-*employés* £300,000.

These figures are certainly very striking, but the development of which they are the measure belongs to co-operative enterprise rather than to the topic of workmen's participation on which we are now specially engaged.

As the upshot of this paper, I wish to make a practical suggestion, viz. that active steps be taken to ascertain whether the persons employed as managers, clerks, salesmen and saleswomen, porters, messengers etc., in co-operative stores may not, with advantage both to the employing establishment and to themselves, be admitted to participation in profits. The great results which have been already attained on the Continent by the application of this system, and which are as yet but very imperfectly known in this country, seem to me of themselves an adequate ground for the inquiry I have ventured to suggest. Exhortation in support of my proposal would be singularly out of place in such a gathering as the present, where I gladly submit it for discussion, confident that English co-operators are the very last people to reject as visionary a beneficent reform which a private French trader has experimentally proved to be feasible.

MEMORANDUM

ON THE

INDUSTRIAL PARTNERSHIP AT THE WHITWOOD
COLLIERIES, NORMANTON, YORKSHIRE

(1865-1874),

BY

ARCHIBALD BRIGGS AND THE LATE HENRY CURRER BRIGGS.

A REVIVED interest having been evinced in the attempt to introduce the principle of Industrial Partnership into Productive Undertakings, and many inquiries having been made as to the circumstances under which that principle was abandoned at these Collieries, we think it advisable to issue a statement showing how the experiment originated, what measure of success attended it, and why after being in operation for a period of nine years it was eventually abandoned.

The following is an impartial record of the facts attending this endeavour to reconcile the interests of Capital and Labour, and it is hoped that it will be useful to those who may hereafter endeavour to solve this problem.

Previously to the 1st of July, 1865, the Whitwood

Collieries were carried on by the private firm of Henry Briggs, Son and Co., and during a period of ten years four strikes occurred, lasting in the aggregate seventy-eight weeks.

The pecuniary effects of these disputes were very serious both to the firm and to their workmen, and a remedy was sought by the introduction of the system of Industrial Partnership.

In November, 1864, a proposal was made that the Company should be registered under the Act of 1862, the plant and stock being taken over at the sum whereat they were valued in the books of the Firm, the Partners stipulating that they should retain two-thirds of the Capital of the Company, and also the full control of the practical management, whilst in the allotment of the remaining one-third a preference should be given to applications for shares from Officials and Operatives employed in the business, and from Customers purchasing the produce of the Collieries.

This was an important stipulation, but the most novel feature of the proposal was introduced by the following clause in the prospectus :—

In order, however, to associate capital and labour still more intimately the founders of the Company will recommend to the shareholders that, whenever the divisible profits accruing from the business shall (after the usual reservation for redemption of capital and other legitimate allowances) exceed ten per cent. on the capital embarked, all those employed by the Company, whether as managers or agents at fixed salaries, or as work-people, shall receive one-half of such excess profit as a bonus, to be distributed amongst them in proportion to, and as a percentage upon, their respective earnings, during the year in which such profits shall have accrued.

It was at the same time explained to the workmen that the current rate of wages paid to the *employés*, and of salary to the Manager, should not exceed the average of remuneration for similar work performed in the same district. It was further arranged that in order to qualify himself for participation in the bonus each workman should purchase, at the cost of one penny, a small book wherein his wages should be entered at stated intervals.

The result of the first year's working enabled the Directors to declare a dividend at the rate of ten per cent., and a bonus of two per cent., on the paid-up Capital, and to appropriate a sum of £1800, being equivalent to two per cent. on the Capital, to the formation of a Labour Bonus Fund for the payment of bonus on the earnings of such of the *employés* of the Company as had qualified themselves to be participants by the fulfilment of the above-named condition.

In making a distribution from the fund thus formed it was thought advisable to accord to workmen who had taken shares in the Company a larger proportion than was paid to those who had not shown their interest and confidence in the concern, and while the former received ten per cent. on the wages they had earned during the year, the latter had only five per cent. Some inequality between the advantages gained by working shareholders and working non-shareholders was continued during the whole time that the system remained in operation.

The following table shows the amount paid in dividend and bonus to shareholders together with the equivalent devoted to the bonus on labour during the following years:—

Year ending	On Capital.		Distributed amongst Employés.
	Dividend.	Bonus.	
		£	£
June 30, 1867	10 per cent.	2700 = to 3 per cent.	2700
,, 1868	10 ,,	3150 = ,, 3½ ,,	3150
,, 1869	10 ,,	3462 = ,, 3½ ,,	3462
,, 1870	10 ,,	1740 = ,, 1¾ ,,	1740
,, 1871	10 ,,	1745 = ,, 1¾ ,,	1745
,, 1872	10 ,,	5250 = ,, 5 ,,	5250

During the last of this series of years the inflation in the coal trade commenced, the prices of coal rising rapidly with a corresponding advance in the rate of wages. The workmen employed by the Company asked and obtained conditional advances on their standard rate of wages amounting in the aggregate to from twenty-seven and a half to thirty per cent., such advances being in addition to participation in the bonus of £5250 as stated above. In granting these advances, the Managers pointed out that it is a fundamental principle of Industrial Partnership that the capitalist is as much entitled to realise a return on his capital equal to the average obtained from similar undertakings as are his workpeople to receive the average rate of wages paid for similar work, and that, as the profits of the coal trade generally had largely increased, the initial rate of interest payable on capital would for the future be augmented in the same ratio as the advance on the standard remuneration of labour. This view was concurred in by the workpeople as a fair arrangement, considering the exceptionally prosperous state of the trade.

During the year ending the 30th of June, 1873, the prices of coal and rate of wages continued to rise, until the latter had increased at least fifty per cent. on the original standard. The initial rate of interest on capital was accordingly raised from ten per cent. to fifteen per cent.

The appropriation of divisible profits realised from the Collieries in the next two years was as follows :—

Year ending	On Capital.		Distributed amongst *Employés*.
	Dividend.	Bonus.	
June 30, 1873	15 per cent.	£ 14,256 = to 10 per cent.	£ 14,256
,, 1874	15 ,,	6,048 = ,, 3 ,,	6,048

During the half-year ending the 31st of December, 1874, the reaction commenced, and the selling prices of coal gradually declined. This change in the trade necessitating a reduction in wages throughout the district, notices to that effect were issued to the miners. The men however declined to recognise this necessity, and the employers thereupon offered to refer the question to arbitration, but it was only after a strike of four weeks' duration, in which the workmen of the Company joined, that this offer of arbitration was accepted. After much negotiation the matter was referred to the decision of Mr. Daniel, Q.C., who finally awarded a considerable reduction.

The strike above referred to caused great dissatisfaction among the outside shareholders who strongly expressed their objection to the continuance of the system of sharing their profits with workpeople who nevertheless still had recourse to the old method of warfare between Capital and Labour, which it was confidently hoped Industrial Partnership had for ever banished. The Directors therefore reluctantly announced that, inasmuch as the Miners act in all questions arising between themselves and their Employers strictly under instructions from the Executive of the Union, it is evident that they are no longer prepared to recognise any special arrangement with the Company. The system of payment of bonus on earnings was consequently thereafter discontinued, although many of the workmen still retained and continue to hold to this day shares in the Company.

Having given this summary of the facts of the case, it is necessary that we should explain more in detail the causes which in our opinion tended to bring about this rupture in the arrangement which for some years had apparently worked so satisfactorily.

A general impression prevails that the workmen of the Company were prohibited from joining the Miners' trades Union. This however is not the fact, although it was hoped that, as industrial partnership gave all that trades Unionism could fairly demand, the workmen would gradually substitute combination *with* their employers for combination *against* them. In order to strengthen the feeling of mutual confidence, we refrained from joining any combination of Employers for the regulation of wages.

Until the summer of 1868 the workmen seemed to enter into these views, but at that time a growing desire to join the Union began to manifest itself, on the ground that as the Company agreed to pay the average weekly wages of the district as well as a share in the profits, and as the Union tended to raise those wages, it was the interest of the workmen to aid in that endeavour.

It was obvious to us that if the men were entitled to join their Union to combine to raise the standard rate of wages, it would become incumbent on us in the interests of our shareholders to combine with other employers in keeping it down, and thus our object in entering into the system of Industrial Partnership would be entirely frustrated.

It was not however until the year 1872 that any actual collision with the Miners' Union took place. After having fixed on the 19th of August in that year as the day on which to hold the annual meeting of the Company, we received a notice stating that a great meeting and demonstration of the Miners' Union was to take place on that day, and that, as our men intended to be present, they requested us to stop work at the pits and give them all a holiday for the purpose. Although no doubt it was an accidental circumstance that our Company and the men's Union should have chosen the same day for their meetings, we felt that we could not consent to the pits being stopped for Union purposes and at considerable cost to our Shareholders on the very day when we were going to ask the latter to grant a bonus to the men of over £5000, on the ground that the Industrial Partnership system caused them to work better than those at the neighbouring Collieries. We felt this the more strongly when we learned that some of those Collieries were to be at work as usual.

A notice was accordingly issued to the effect that any workman absenting himself from work in order to attend the Union meeting would be considered as forfeiting all claim to bonus for the future. About one-third of the men did so forfeit their bonus, and their wages were no longer entered in the bonus books until the succeeding Christmas, when, there having been no further difficulty, they were once more admitted to participation as before.

Up to this time (1872) our Company had not united with the other Colliery Proprietors in the consideration of any questions relating to wages, but when a joint Committee of masters and men was formed we joined in promoting it, believing it to be a good means of settling minor points of difference which might otherwise lead to strikes.

About this time the great advances in the selling prices of coal commenced, and wages also rose very considerably. It is useless now to discuss the vexed question as to whether the rise in prices caused that of wages or *vice versâ;* no doubt the *initiative* was taken by the Coal-Masters in raising prices, and when the ball was once set rolling it was kept in motion by a largely increased demand for coal, combined with a diminution of production, as the higher wages of the men tended to make them less eager to exert themselves to secure a large output, their wages being paid on the tonnage produced. The new rules and precautions enforced by the "Mines' Regulation Act" also added to the cost of production.

No doubt wages and prices thus acted and reacted on each other and while coal-owners' profits and miners' wages increased the public suffered.

During the extraordinarily prosperous financial year ending on the 30th of June, 1873, all went apparently well, but the rift in the lute was no doubt in reality gradually widening. Some of the surrounding Colliery Proprietors, anxious to attract men to their pits and secure as large a share as possible of the great prosperity, and finding the bonus given by our Company was a great inducement to men to remain with us, began to offer something beyond the regular wages of the district, saying it was "instead of Briggs' bonus," thus strengthening the view already entertained by some discontented men that the bonus was something kept back out of the weekly wages to be given at the end of the year, and that if we could pay it *then* we could give it to them weekly just as well. The very magnitude of the sums divided among the men, though rendering the Industrial Partnership principle very popular for the time, yet to a certain extent contributed to its failure, rendering the smaller bonus subsequently paid less appreciated; while the very large amounts that could be earned as weekly wages also made the Colliery operatives think less of the advantages we offered.

During all this period small issues of shares were made at less than the market value to workmen exclusively, and the latter were encouraged and aided by means of share clubs to take them up.

As during the year 1874 the great prosperity of the coal trade began to wane an unfortunate cause of difference arose, to explain which we must again refer to a period previous to that of which we have been speaking.

Before the very good times the men had always been required to riddle or sift the coal in the pits, to separate and leave below ground the very small dust or "smudge" which was not saleable. As the payment for coal-getting is by the weight brought to the surface, this involved the loss of wages on the small percentage of coal consequently left in the pits, as well as some extra labour.

When the great demand for coal arose, however, even this smudge was saleable, and we proposed for a time to dispense with riddles. A kind of representative meeting of men was called, at which it was agreed that during the very good times they might send up the coal unriddled with all the dust in it on consideration of a reduction of one penny per ton on the wages. At the same time they were told that when the trade returned to its normal condition, as no doubt it would sooner or later, they must be prepared to return to the former system.

This was agreed to by all present as only reasonable, and so the matter was settled on terms that appeared satisfactory to all parties. At length, however, as the great demand for fuel began to decline, we found it was impossible to sell the smudge and were compelled to give fourteen days' notice to the men that they must carry out the understanding and again use the riddles, we on our side returning the penny per ton which had been agreed upon as an equivalent. A Deputation, however, waited upon the Managing Director (at that time Archibald Briggs) who was informed that the men meant never again to submit to use riddles. After some rather warm discussion fourteen days' further grace was accorded, in order that a general meeting of the men employed at the Collieries might be held to reconsider the matter, and in view of the advances that had taken place in wages since one penny per ton had been settled upon as the equivalent in money for the use of riddles, one penny three farthings was proposed as the allowance. Eventually the Managing Director attended a general meeting of the men when over a thousand were present, and with considerable difficulty obtained a hearing. He pointed out how thoroughly the Company had kept faith with them, and divided about £34,000 among them as bonus in the course of eight years, and appealed to them strongly to fulfil the agreement by which they were in honour bound.

These arguments were most distasteful to the assembled workmen, who vociferously refused to hear one of their body who alone ventured to try to speak in favour of them, and a written resolution was handed up headed "West Yorkshire Miners' Union, Normanton Lodge" expressing determination never again to submit to the introduction of riddles. This resolution was finally passed with only three or four dissentients. The Managing Director pointed out to the men that this resolution by which the Miners' Union came between the Company and their workmen would prove the death-blow to Industrial Partnership—that the men in effect thus declined any longer to treat with us individually, and could not expect our large body of shareholders to be willing to accord to them exceptional advantages which they were evidently no longer prepared to reciprocate.

Finally the question of the use of riddles was referred to the Joint Committee of masters and men, which decided that the arrangement made by the representative men attending the small meeting first alluded to was not to be considered as binding on the whole body of workmen, inasmuch as there had been no written agreement drawn up. This decision was accepted by the Company, though it seemed rather hard upon them inasmuch as the arrangement was eagerly adopted and acted upon as long as it was in favour of the men, and only repudiated when the old system of working, which it was intended temporarily to abolish, was to be resumed. The still further downward movement in trade, however, eventually convinced even the men of the necessity of submitting to the use of riddles when required, with a payment of one penny halfpenny per ton as compensation.

It is only justice to say that it afterwards transpired that many men not belonging to our Collieries obtained admittance to the disorderly mass meeting, actuated by the knowledge that our decision on the matter to be discussed would probably affect that of other Colliery owners.

The events above described did not, however, lead at once to the abolition of the Industrial Partnership system. At the meeting of Shareholders held in August, 1874, it was decided not entirely to abandon it, but to give it one more chance, modifying however the rules regulating the distribution of the bonus, and making those rules more stringent. It was not until the Company's pits were, in common with others in the district, laid idle for four weeks in the strike against the inevitable reduction of wages, that the final step was taken, and a resolution passed at the half-yearly meeting of Shareholders held in February, 1875, that the payment of a bonus on the Industrial Partnership principle should be discontinued. Many of the men themselves had expressed a wish to the same effect, having an idea that we were in some way merely keeping back a portion of their wages to be probably (but not certainly) returned to them at the end of the year; and they said they would prefer to be paid precisely the same wages, and be put on the same footing as men at other Collieries.

Thus ended the experiment which a year or two before had appeared to promise such great success.

From the time when the resolution was adopted by which the Industrial Partnership system at the Whitwood Collieries became a thing of the past up to the present period, the trade has been in such a depressed state that, had that system still been in force, there would never have been any available balance for division among the workmen and the question indeed would have arisen: If Labour is allowed to participate in all profits after the payment of a certain fixed percentage on Capital, should it not also help to make good any deficiency when the state of trade does not allow of that fixed percentage being earned, and in this case how is this end to be attained?

Having now traced shortly the history of the experiment and the causes of its failure as far as we

K

can judge of them, it only remains to say that nothing that has occurred seems to show that the system inaugurated at Whitwood may not eventually be generally and successfully adopted, and lead to a more intimate union of interests and a more cordial feeling between capitalists and their workmen ; but to succeed it must be carried out honourably and with perfect confidence and good faith on both sides. If acted on thoroughly, great changes in the rate of wages should never take place. Both Capital and Labour should be satisfied with a moderate and unvarying return in the first instance, and be prepared to wait for any further remuneration until the balancing of accounts at the end of the year. As long as working men remain in a position necessitating an immediate payment for their labour, and cannot by habits of prudence and self-control afford to wait until it fructifies, they cannot expect employers as a rule to treat Labour otherwise than as a commodity, to be bought at the lowest possible price, subject only to the ordinary laws of supply and demand.

The advance in the wages of the Colliery operatives which took place during the years 1872 and 1873 was so great that any probable bonus became comparatively insignificant in their eyes, and they are not yet sufficiently educated to understand the full value of the Industrial Partnership system, as leading them to something higher than working for mere fixed weekly wages.

Many of our workmen still continue to be shareholders in the concern, and we trust that, even though the endeavour to avoid all cause of disputes on the question of wages by a union of interests has failed for the present, at any rate the times are past when violence and threats were resorted to. If our Company and its men must be antagonists on points where their interests clash, may they at any rate be antagonists who fight fairly and respect each other.

The foregoing is the substance of a Paper originally drawn up by me, and revised by my brother, Mr. H. Currer Briggs, in the year 1875, in order to place on record the facts relating to the establishment, subsequent working and ultimate abandonment of the system of Industrial Partnership at the Whitwood Collieries.

That Paper has never hitherto been made public, and was in course of revision by my brother when his unfortunate and sudden death took place on the 21st of October last. I have since his death completed the revision and can confidently say that, although, he being no longer among us, his name cannot be appended, I know the statement as it stands embodies his carefully considered views as well as my own.

I may be allowed to add that my Brother was the originator of the idea of establishing a Limited Company expressly in order to carry out the experiment of interesting the workmen in the concern, and from its formation in 1865 he was the Managing Director and I myself the Secretary until the death of our Father, Mr. Henry Briggs, in 1868. From that time my Brother was the Chairman and I took the post of Managing Director until the year 1876, when, the health of my family compelling me to reside abroad, he undertook the duties of both positions, and fulfilled them up to the time of his death, assisted by his son, Mr. Arthur Currer Briggs, who has now been appointed the Managing Director in his place.

I give this information merely to show that the practical management of the concern was in our hands during the whole time over which the experiment extended, and I can only say in conclusion that throughout that time we both of us endeavoured as far as in us lay to deal fairly by both the large interests confided to our care—that of the Workmen as well as that of the Shareholders—and to give the experiment whose history is here related every chance of success.

ARCHIBALD BRIGGS.

WHITWOOD COLLIERY, NORMANTON,
8th December, 1881.

REMARKS ON
MESSRS. BRIGGS' MEMORANDUM.

BY SEDLEY TAYLOR.

THE experiment described in the foregoing Memorandum attracted, from its very commencement, an extraordinary amount of public interest. Immediate publicity was given to it by statements which Messrs. Briggs communicated to the Social Science Association in 1866, and gave in evidence before the Royal Commission on Trades Unions in 1868. The strong language of approval held concerning the experiment, while its success was still unimpaired, in the writings of Mill, Fawcett and Thornton, gave to it a still wider notoriety and caused the most sanguine expectations to be founded on the continued prosperity augured for the system. When the abandonment of Profit-Sharing at the Whitwood Collieries became publicly known the feeling of disappointment and discouragement was therefore proportionately widespread. The hopes of persons friendly to the system received a severe blow, and its enemies at once eagerly assumed that "abandonment" and "failure" necessarily meant the same thing.

It was thus urgently desirable in the interests

of the participating principle that an authoritative account of the nature and causes of the collapse should be promptly forthcoming, and the absence of such an account, especially when contrasted with the full information spontaneously offered when the experiment was working satisfactorily, gave rise to injurious suspicions that the inner history of the Whitwood experiment would not bear examination.

The reasons which both then and subsequently enjoined silence on Messrs. Briggs are, however, perfectly clear. They had to carry on the business of the Whitwood Collieries in their own interest and in that of the other shareholders. If, in the exasperated state of feeling necessarily consequent on the abandonment of Industrial Partnership, they had come before the public with an unreserved statement, they would inevitably have involved themselves in a regular campaign of recrimination with their own workmen which might easily have paralysed their whole undertaking.

Somewhat later the introduction of the "sliding-scale" for regulating the rate of wages rendered the time inopportune for reviving memories of conflict.

It was only when this arrangement had been got into steady operation that Mr. Henry Currer Briggs judged the moment come for taking the public into his entire confidence. To him belongs the honour of having been the earliest pioneer of Profit-Sharing in Great Britain, of having preserved, even though defeated in its service, an unshaken faith in its ultimate triumph, and of having chronicled his own experience with the most honourable frankness.

It is satisfactory to learn that his deserts are recognised by the Whitwood miners, who have by spontaneous subscription among themselves placed a memorial on his grave. The confidence shown by him to an almost entire stranger, in entrusting the publication of so interesting and important a Memorandum to my hands, I here gratefully acknowledge.

On the materials which it supplies, and some others collected elsewhere, I propose to examine what beneficial results were attained under Industrial Partnership at Whitwood, and whether the reasons assigned for the decision taken by the Company to terminate their great experiment, suffice to justify a step the seriously discouraging effect of which on the future of Profit-Sharing could not have been for a moment doubtful.

Participation was introduced at Whitwood as a remedy for trade conflicts of extraordinary duration. In the ten years ending the 1st of July, 1865, there occurred strikes lasting in the aggregate a year and a half. Evidence of the hatred and distrust felt by the colliers towards their employer during this period is preserved to us in the pages of Thornton and of the Trades Union Commissioners' Report. "All coalmasters is devils, and Briggs is the prince of devils," said one of them: "He would be the devil if he only had horns," said another who afterwards saw reason to change his opinion. The following extract from an anonymous letter will show that the miners were far from concealing the nature of their sentiments from the object of them :—

Mr. Briggs I will tell you what i think by you about this struggle ... you shall not Live 13 days. Depend on it my nife is sharp but my bulits is shorer than the nife ... and if it be at noon wen I see you you shall have the arra if it be in your charit like old Abe.* Now reade that and pray to God to forgive you your sins to be reddy.

In short the feeling towards Messrs. Briggs before the introduction of participation was, to use the words of a miner examined before the Royal Commission, "as bad as it could be," and in 1863 it had broken out in a riot followed by the conviction of some of the ringleaders at the York Assizes.

It is plain that such an atmosphere of ingrained distrust was highly unfavourable to the effective working of the participatory principle, to which mutual confidence is as the life-blood. Accordingly we find that principle from the outset regarded with suspicion by particular sections of the men.

By some it was believed to be instituted in order to "destroy the Union." Others agreed with a miner cited by Thornton who remarked "The thing is good, but you see it comes from Briggs, and I have no faith in Briggs." Notwithstanding these suspicions the experiment produced during the first three years of its continuance excellent results both material and moral, as is abundantly clear from statements made by Messrs. H. C. & A. Briggs and their *employés* before the Trades Union Commission in 1868.† It is worth while to set out this evidence with some fulness.

MR. H. C. BRIGGS told the Royal Commissioners he was sure there had been a large saving in the item of rails. Men

---

* King Ahab (1 Kings ii. 34).
† Sessional Papers, 1867-8, vol. xli. pp. 46, *sqq.*

used to break a new rail to get it the right length and then perhaps repeat the process if unsuccessful, burying the one first broken in the coal-dirt. Nothing of the kind occurred any longer. He believed the colliers worked more, and more economically, than before, though statistical evidence of this was difficult to procure. The stoppages of work for frivolous reasons, formerly so common, now scarcely ever occurred. He found that the collieries worked " infinitely more smoothly " than under the old system, and that the men were much better under control and far more amenable to reason.

MR. ARCHIBALD BRIGGS was decidedly of opinion that there was a great improvement morally and intellectually. The new Rector of Normanton, Mr. Lane, had on coming there remarked a great difference as to character in favour of Messrs. Briggs' men over miners employed in other collieries who lived almost in the same row of houses. He found them a better and steadier set of men, and as a new-comer did not understand whence the difference arose. Out of a thousand men who received bonus at the same time only three were known to have stayed away from work and drunk it up. These were dismissed amidst general approval. The number of children sent to school had very largely increased.

MR. J. PYRAH, working pitman, gave evidence as follows :— " I believe that in this system we have found a remedy for strikes and lock-outs. The feeling is quite altered. There is a hostile feeling yet which will take years, I believe, to cure, but we are progressing and things are widely different from what they were two years ago." His own life had, he added, been rendered " very much happier " by the new system.

MR. J. PICKLES, store-keeper, who had been Secretary to the Miners' Union during the strike of 1858, said it was a very common expression when picking up a large nail to say " This is so much bonus saved." The men in the pit would sometimes get out a difficult prop which they might under other circumstances have left, saying " That is so much saved towards bonus." He believed that feeling was becoming more general.

MR. JOHN TOFT, working collier, said :—" The scheme has done a vast amount of good : it has destroyed a vast amount of ill feeling, and I have not the slightest doubt that by perseverance and so forth it will have the effect of bringing the whole of the men round to our side" (*i.e.* that of the friends of the new system). He considered it "had already done a deal of good" in encouraging industrious and provident habits. "Men that were reckless and drunken and such like have begun to improve." He was confident that there was a better feeling between employer and employed.

The zeal of this witness for Profit-Sharing had stood the test of personal maltreatment. He attended a meeting of miners at which a Union lecturer denounced Messrs. Briggs' system as a device for "cheating the men." "When he had finished," Mr. Toft told the Commissioners, "I got up to defend the principle because it is dear to my life. I believe it is a good thing and is calculated to do good and I have taken it up not for any amount of interest or flattery or benefit I might get from the Masters by advocating it, but because I believe it is destined to do a great amount of good. They would not let me continue to speak, and overpowered my voice, and I had a clod come at my head."

(MR. ROEBUCK. "I hope it did not strike you.")

"It did not hurt me, only my feelings were hurt."

In 1866, Mr. Archibald Briggs made the following statement before the Social Science Association:—

Our detailed monthly estimates of profit and loss have brought out a rather curious confirmation of the value and correctness of the views we hold; on comparing the respective profits yielded by each of the three seams of coal we are working, it appears that those profits (other things being equal) increase in a tolerably exact proportion to the number of workmen who interest themselves in our co-operative movement.*

The evidence adduced above shows that during the first three years of the experiment the stimulus of Profit-Sharing was successful in eliciting improved production and smoother industrial relations. As it appeared important to ascertain how far these advantages were subsequently maintained, I requested from Mr. Archibald Briggs supplemental information on

* *i.e.* the Industrial Partnership.

this point which had not been referred to in the Memorandum. He replied as follows :—

In regard to whether any pecuniary advantage was gained by the Shareholders of the Company in consequence of the establishment of the Industrial Partnership system,—whether in fact had that system not been adopted, the dividends paid would have been less or more than were actually paid, it is very difficult to judge. My own opinion is that down to the 30th of June, 1872, the Shareholders did reap a benefit, but that the enormous rise in selling prices in the season of inflation altered the whole circumstances, and that during the succeeding two years the bonus paid to workmen was more than was earned by any extra care and steady work given by the latter.

You ask also whether the freedom from strikes enjoyed can be fairly attributed to the Industrial Partnership system. This cannot be affirmed to be altogether the case, inasmuch as during the whole of the time it was in force no general strikes took place in our district, but certainly we were more exempt from partial and temporary cessations of work owing to disputes and grievances than were the other Colliery owners of the district, and our men were more ready to accommodate themselves to the exigencies of the trade, working extra hours when circumstances rendered this important in the interests of the business, in a way they had never done before.

I do not however myself consider that any isolated concern adopting the Industrial Partnership principle can ever expect to reap the full benefits to be derived therefrom. Its great advantages can only be secured by its becoming general and gradually altering the whole tone of the relations between employer and employed, doing away with antagonistic combinations of one class against the other, and destroying the last remnants of the old feeling among the workmen, already I trust dying out in consequence of better education, that somehow anything tending to the disadvantage of the employer must be their gain.

Only by the working man becoming thoroughly a partner with his employer, dependent for his welfare upon the success of the undertaking in which both are engaged, and this not merely in isolated cases but throughout the length and breadth of the land, can the full benefit of the Industrial Partnership system be realised.

Data have now been furnished for roughly estimating the material and moral results attained by Profit-Sharing at the Whitwood Collieries. An examination of the history of the experiment as set forth in Messrs. Briggs' Memorandum, to which I next proceed, will, I believe, satisfy the reader that no adequate reasons have been there assigned for the withdrawal of the system. That, under the exceptional and singularly untoward surroundings of the experiment, decisions were taken by the Company which subsequent experience has shown to have been errors of judgment, reflects no discredit on the administrative capacity of their advisers, who were directing a novel enterprise without this light to guide them. That working pitmen, too, should not have at once grasped the central principle on which depends the successful working of participatory industry, can as little be made matter of charge against them, especially when it is remembered that even the Royal Commissioners on Trades Unions, after having heard very full evidence from Messrs. Briggs as to the system pursued at Whitwood, reported on that system in terms which showed that they had essentially misunderstood its mode of operation.*

* The following passage appears in the Commissioners' Report:— "As regards Messrs. Briggs' system the principle is to limit the profits of the employer and to give to the workman over and above his wages, a share in the profits of the concern without subjecting him to any liability for loss. It is then not unreasonable to suppose that many capitalists will prefer the chances of disputes with their workmen, and even run the risk of strikes and temporary loss, rather than voluntarily *limit their profits to ten per cent. or any other fixed amount.*" (Sessional Papers, 1868–9, vol. xxxvi., p. 28.)

Messrs. Briggs never proposed to limit their profits to a fixed

I propose to take *seriatim* the principal incidents narrated in the Memorandum as having led up to the abandonment of Profit-Sharing, and to discuss them with entire freedom called for alike by the importance of the experiment and by the high character and meritorious personal exertions of the gentlemen who conducted it.

The usually somewhat invidious privilege of wisdom after the event I gladly accept in the hope of turning it to account for the future progress of Profit-Sharing.

The very important step taken in 1873 by which the rate of interest payable on capital, prior to any division of profits, was raised from ten to fifteen per cent. shall first be considered. It will be remembered that the Managers, when giving notice of this change in 1872, pointed out "that it is a fundamental principle of Industrial Partnership that the capitalist is as much entitled to realise a return on his capital equal to the average obtained from similar undertakings as are his workpeople to receive the average rate of wages paid for similar work, and that as the profits of the coal trade generally had largely increased, the initial rate of interest payable on capital would for the future be augmented in the same ratio as the advance on the standard remuneration of labour."

amount as stated in the passage which I have placed in italics. They fixed, indeed, a limit below which no profits would be assigned to their *employés*, but they shared with the latter all profits exceeding that limit. The point that a new source of profits is opened by giving to workmen a direct interest in the results of their labour evidently altogether escaped Her Majesty's Commissioners.

The Memorandum goes on to say that "this view was concurred in by the workpeople as a fair arrangement considering the exceptionally prosperous state of the trade."

I must dispute the position here taken up by the Managers in regarding as "a fundamental principle of Industrial Partnership" that the initial interest payable on capital should be made to vary with the fluctuations of current wages. The practice in participating houses whose regulations are publicly accessible is I believe invariably—certainly in the great majority of instances—to keep this interest at one unchanging rate.*

The expedient of making the rate of interest on capital vary with that of wages thus finds no support in the ordinary practice of Industrial Partnership. That it introduced a radical change into the system on which that principle had been at work at Whitwood since 1864 is clear from the clause in the Company's prospectus of that year,† announcing that equal division of surplus profits between capital and labour would be recommended to the shareholders whenever, subject to ordinary reservations, the divisible profits exceeded ten per cent. on the capital embarked.

With regard to the alteration itself there can be no question that the Company were perfectly entitled to make it. No stipulation in reference to, nor even mention of, the Industrial Partnership appeared in their Articles of Association, and they had full power

---

* In the case of Herr von Thünen's farm (*ante*, p. 90) a change of regulation in favour of capital was, it is true, made, but the alteration was not considerable in amount and occurred but once during an experiment of long duration.

† See *ante* p. 118.

to modify or abolish it at their pleasure. In what light, as a question of expediency, the step actually taken is to be regarded must mainly depend on whether preponderating importance is attributed to the immediate pecuniary interests of the shareholders or to the prospects of the industrial experiment then on its trial.

During the six years preceding the period of inflation the shareholders' total dividends averaged twelve and a half per cent. per annum on their capital. In 1872, when the minimum interest still stood at ten per cent., their dividend was fifteen per cent. on capital. Had the Company held to this arrangement in 1873 and 1874, the dividends for those years would have been twenty-two and a half per cent. and fifteen per cent. respectively. The change actually made brought them up to twenty-five per cent. and eighteen per cent., while it reduced the share in profits accruing to labour from £17,820 to £14,256 in 1873, and from £11,088 to £6048 in 1874.*

---

* The division of profits which would have taken place in 1873 and 1874 had the original arrangement continued in force, is deduced as follows from the figures given on p. 121 :—

In **1873** the share-capital was ten times the bonus paid, or £142,560. The net profits consisted of twenty-five per cent. on capital + the bonus to labour. They amounted therefore to $\frac{1}{4} \times £142,560 + £14,256$ = £35,640 + £14,256 = £49,896.

Under the ten-per-cent. limit, the initial interest due to capital would have been $\frac{1}{10} \times £142,560$, or £14,256, and the amount available for division between capital and labour £49,896 − £14,256 = £35,640. The bonus to each would therefore have been one-half this, or £17,820.

The shareholders would, therefore, have received in all £14,256

When we bear in mind amidst what feelings of extreme suspicion and hostility on the part of the workmen towards their employers the system of Industrial Partnership was introduced at Whitwood, it seems hardly possible to doubt that the action taken by the Company in altering the terms of Profit-Sharing must have been regarded by their *employés* as manifesting a determination to appropriate too large a share of the great prosperity. The fact of the workmen having concurred in the new arrangement when it was announced in 1872 would not prevent a bitter feeling arising when they saw the bonus to labour cut down from £17,820 to £14,250 in 1873, in order that the Company might divide twenty-five per cent. instead of twenty-two and a half per cent., and from £11,088 to £6048 in 1874, in order that the shareholders' dividend might be eighteen instead of fifteen per cent.

I wish here explicitly to guard myself against being understood as expressing any opinion upon the merits of the Company's decision. I do not possess the data on which to form such an opinion. All I

+ £17,820 = £32,076, which on a total capital of £142,560 is almost exactly **twenty-two and a half per cent.** The bonus to labour, as just seen, would have been **£17,820.**

In **1874** the share-capital was $\frac{100}{3}$ × £6048 = £201,600. The net profits amounted to eighteen per cent. on capital + the bonus to labour = £36,288 + £6048 = £42,336.

Initial interest at ten per cent. on capital would have brought the shareholders £20,160, and left for equal division between them and the workmen £42,336 − £20,160 = £22,176. The shareholders' dividend would therefore have been £20,160 + £11,088 = £31,248, which is **fifteen per cent.** on a capital of £201,600. The bonus to labour would have been **£11,088.**

say is that their action was, on the face of it, likely to arouse the resentment of their *employés*, and, by thus reviving the old feelings of hostility, very seriously to prejudice the future of their participatory experiment.

I come next to the relations between the Company and the Trade Union which play so important a part in the sequence of events. The first actual collision occurred in 1872, when the Union announced a great miners' demonstration on the day which Messrs. Briggs had already fixed for the annual meeting of their shareholders. The men requested that work might be stopped at the pits and that they might have a holiday in order to attend the Union meeting. The reply of the Managers was a notice to the effect that any man absenting himself from work for that purpose would be considered as forfeiting all claim to bonus for the future. About one-third of the men set the notice at defiance and were excluded from profit-sharing, but readmitted to it three months afterwards, as no further difficulty had meanwhile arisen.

This would appear to have been one of those untoward fortuitous conjunctures which are often more difficult to deal with than deliberately hostile acts. The coincidence in date of the two meetings was admittedly accidental, but, assuming that adequate reasons stood in the way of a subsequent change of day on either side, it undoubtedly constituted a serious difficulty. Messrs. Briggs were desirous of demonstrating to their shareholders the virtue of Industrial Partnership in eliciting greater zeal and improved work. Nothing could be more mortifying for them than to have to replace this demonstration by an exhi-

L

bition of activity totally suspended—pits absolutely deserted for Trade Union purposes. The Managers may have even doubted whether the shareholders, with this evidence before their eyes, would consent to vote an unprecedentedly heavy bonus to labour proposed to them on the ground of the superior activity called forth by Profit-Sharing. In this emergency they may have felt that a determined exertion of authority was imperatively called for in the ultimate interest of the participating workmen themselves. We are not informed whether Messrs. Briggs, before resorting to the threat of deprivation, explained to the men the manifest advisability of conciliating the shareholders by working on the day of meeting. Provided, however, that this obvious course was tried and failed of its object, the measure actually adopted, autocratic as it undoubtedly was, may have been the best move on the board.

The unionist workmen on their side had strong reasons for wishing to attend the meeting of the Miners' Association. There had existed among them from the outset a suspicion that it was one object of Messrs. Briggs' scheme " to draw them away from the trades unions to which they belonged." * They would naturally desire to show by their presence at the Union meeting that no such effect had been produced upon them. Absence from it would point them out to their fellows as " black sheep " whom their own advantages had made selfishly indifferent to the interests of less fortunate comrades in the neighbouring collieries.

* Mr. Lloyd Jones before the Society of Arts, 16th of February, 1881.

While thus there appears to be no ground for complaint in the action of either party, the result of this incident must none the less have been embitterment on the men's part. They would regard Messrs. Briggs' prohibition, and the penal consequences attached to disregard of it, as an unwarrantable interference with their freedom of action. Hostility would thus receive a fresh stimulus, and the foundation of mutual confidence, on which Industrial Partnership can alone rest securely, be further undermined.

The dispute about the "riddles" had no bearing on Profit-Sharing except the unfortunate one of keeping up exasperated feeling. In estimating the amount of censure which should fall on the men for not fulfilling the engagement to resume sifting the coal, the circumstances under which it was made and broken must be taken into account.

There seems room for doubt whether those who entered into the compact with Messrs. Briggs were really authorised to pledge the honour of the whole body of workmen. The agreement was made at "a kind of representative meeting of men"—language which certainly implies that the representation was not of a very formal and binding character. Further, the body which declined to recognise the compact was to a considerable extent composed of different persons from those on whose behalf it was accepted. During the year ending the 30th of June, 1874, the number of participating workmen increased from 1937 to 2218.* Allowing for the corresponding increase

* I owe these figures to the kindness of Mr. Arthur C. Briggs, the present Managing Director at Whitwood.

during the previous year, I shall be within the mark in estimating that, of the men who repudiated the riddling compact, one in seven had never been, in any sense, a party to it. To these considerations must be added the fact, stated with so much frankness in the Memorandum, that many men not belonging to the Whitwood Collieries improperly obtained admittance to the disorderly mass meeting which decided against resuming the use of riddles.

The limitations which I have pointed out constitute, of course, neither excuse nor palliation for the conduct of those workmen—and they must have been not a few—who, having deliberately accepted Messrs. Briggs' terms, assisted in repudiating them at the mass meeting, either from selfish motives or under trade union pressure. It is also clear, apart from all considerations of contract, that to insist on bringing to the pit's mouth small coal which was unsaleable when it got there indicated a gross misconception of the principle of Profit-Sharing. On the whole, therefore, the men's conduct on the riddles dispute appears to have been distinctly blamable.

The warning addressed to the men by Messrs. Briggs that the resolution against all return to the use of riddles, by which the Miners' Union "came between the Company and their workmen," would prove the death-blow to Industrial Partnership may be advantageously considered in conjunction with the final abandonment of that system in 1875 by vote of the shareholders in consequence of the four weeks' strike ordered by the Miners' Union against reduction of wages. I will endeavour to indicate what seems to me to be the point of view from which these crucially important matters should be regarded.

That it is an essential object of Profit-Sharing to establish harmonious relations between capital and labour is so obvious that the system will have to stand or fall according as it proves, or does not prove, capable of preventing, or at least of very effectively discouraging, the occurrence of conflicts between these two agents of industry. The same thing may be said of its capacity to free the heads and workmen of participating houses from all occasion for submitting to unwelcome orders issued by an extraneous association, whether consisting of employers or of employed.

Trade conflicts and dictation *ab extra* are, however, merely symptoms of a deeper-seated industrial malady, and can therefore be permanently got rid of only by a remedy capable of attacking the disease itself in its originating cause. That cause is evidently the widespread and profoundly erroneous conviction that the interests of employers and employed are in the nature of things essentially opposed to each other. Profit-Sharing attacks this root-evil in the most effective way, not by arguing against it, but by setting in active operation a system of remunerating labour based on the opposite doctrine. When *employés* have become convinced that the machinery of this system necessarily brings to them in virtue of its very construction a satisfactory portion of the net profits annually accruing, there will no longer be any motive for spasmodic efforts to drive up wages in order to secure some share of a perhaps but fleeting prosperity. Similarly, when all are directly interested in the results of production, and in improving to the utmost the technical processes by which it is carried on, the practice of seeking to control these processes by regulations emanating from an external body will naturally fall into desuetude. These great results, however, can be looked for only when extensive applications of the profit-sharing principle shall have won for it a strong body of public opinion. As Mr. Archibald Briggs has said with so much force, "its great advantages can only be secured by its becoming general and gradually altering the whole tone of the relations between employer and employed, doing away with antagonistic combinations of one class against the other, and destroying the last remnants of the old feeling among the workmen, already I trust dying out in consequence of better education, that somehow anything tending to the disadvantage of the employer must be their gain."

Let us apply the above general considerations to the Whitwood experiment, made at a time when the principle of mutual antagonism was powerfully and militantly organised, while Industrial Partnership, on the contrary, presented for Great Britain an all but unheard-of novelty. It is plain that these conditions called for the utmost forbearance in dealing with a group of working miners brought up in the atmosphere and inheriting the traditions of bitter class-hostility. Provided evidences of amelioration were not absolutely wanting, occasional outbreaks of the antagonistic spirit, whether taking the form of Union interference or of actual strike, formed no more reason for abandoning the experiment than the occurrence of relapses during the treatment of a serious disease is a ground for throwing up the case as hopeless. An error of judgment appears, therefore, to have been committed in publicly prognosticating destruction to Industrial Partnership from the action taken by the Miners' Union in the riddling dispute, and still more in finally abandoning the profit-sharing principle because the *employés* of the Company did not hold aloof from the general strike ordered by their trade society.

Had the Company allowed the participatory arrangement to remain in force, the ensuing period of depression would, it is true, have prevented the assignment of any bonus to labour. Such a cessation would, however, have been recognised as being merely a local misfortune consequent upon unavoidable vicissitudes of industry. The step actually taken was interpreted as involving an admission by the authors of the Whitwood experiment that the principle of Industrial Partnership itself had proved a failure. As things turned out, there was manifestly no occasion for this extreme measure. Had on the contrary business revived, and the system been retained, the next division of surplus profits would have offered an excellent opportunity for making the men practically aware of the loss entailed by the strike, in diminished returns, upon themselves as well as upon the shareholders.

The foregoing remarks having been laid before Mr. Archibald Briggs, he was kind enough to write me the following letter which will assist the reader in forming a fair judgment on the issues now raised in reference to the Whitwood experiment :—

MY DEAR SIR,

Many thanks for allowing me to see the manuscript of your remarks regarding the abandonment of the "Industrial Partnership" or "Profit-Sharing" system at the Whitwood Collieries. I will only trouble you with a very few observations thereon.

In the first place I would say that you naturally express your views from the standpoint of an outsider, whose pecuniary position is in no way at stake. We, and the other Directors, whose action you criticise were all largely interested, and in the case of some of us the future of ourselves and our families depended largely upon the success of the undertaking. We felt also that we were responsible to a large body of outside shareholders, many of whom had placed in our hands the hardly earned savings of years, confiding in our capacity and discretion; and the great majority of whom cared little for our experiment except in so far as it might increase or diminish their own dividends. Much therefore as we desired to solve the great social problem in which the whole world was interested, our *first* duty was to our shareholders, and we could take such steps only as obtained their approval and sanction.

Having thus pointed out the difference which I think should be borne in mind between our position as leading actors in the incidents on which you comment, and yours as an outside critic long after those incidents occurred, I would only ask to be allowed to make a few remarks on two of those incidents.

First in regard to the raising of the initial dividend on capital to fifteen per cent. in 1873. I grant that in announcing the change we should have said that the "fundamental principle of Industrial Partnership *as explained in the Prospectus of, and adopted by, this Company*—is that Capital is as much entitled to realise," etc. I have not at hand a copy of the prospectus and am therefore trusting to memory in saying that we therein stated that the wages paid should be the average of those of the district, and the initial profit paid on Capital before the division between Capital and Labour should be the average realised by similar undertakings.* On this understanding the

---

* For the exact terms used in the clause of the prospectus here referred to, see *ante*, p. 118.

principle was adopted at Whitwood, and I still maintain that when wages had been raised some seventy per cent., and we had reason to believe that other collieries in the district were realising increased profits in at least an equal proportion, we were justified in increasing by fifty per cent. the initial dividend on Capital. I feel certain that you are wrong in supposing that this action aroused any adverse feeling among the men. All acknowledged its justice, and I do not remember hearing of any one who objected to so reasonable a proposal. I have not here * the exact figures, but I believe I am not going beyond the mark in saying that the aggregate advances in miners' wages amounted to some seventy per cent. upon those paid in 1870, and had we in 1873 proposed to retain the initial return payable to shareholders at its original figure of ten per cent., and to give our men, in *addition* to their greatly increased wages, half of *all* the extra profit realised from the greatly advanced selling prices of coal, our shareholders would certainly have objected (and I must say I think justly so), and we might have found ourselves outvoted at the annual meeting. I must therefore maintain my opinion that such an attempt to let the men both eat their own cake and have an unfair share of that of the Capitalists would have been both unwise and unjust.

You, I think, grant that if Industrial Partnership is to be adopted generally it must be shown that under it a larger return can be secured by Capital than under the old system. If however we had not in 1873 made the modification to which you demur, our shareholders would have justly felt that their profits were being diminished in order that the miners' already large earnings might be unduly increased.

Secondly in regard to the final abandonment of the System. I must agree with you that, *as things have turned out*, we might as well have continued it. Never since it was given up has the initial dividend of ten per cent. been realised, and had not the system been actually abandoned it would have remained naturally in abeyance. A time we trust will come when the gradually increasing consumption of coal, having overtaken the enormously enlarged production which has of late years swamped the market, the business will again become fairly remunerative. The system

---

* Mr. Briggs resides in Italy.

might then have had a chance of coming again (equally naturally) into active operation. It is easier however to be now, as you say, wise after the event, than it was in 1873 to foresee what the future was to bring forth, and to guide our actions accordingly. A strong feeling prevailed among our shareholders that our men by their action in throwing themselves into the ranks of the Union, and resorting once more to the warfare of strikes, had abandoned on their side the system from which they had so largely benefited ; and we could not but agree with great regret that no course seemed open to us but that of announcing that Industrial Partnership was no longer in force. The above remarks I leave in your hands to do with as you think best, and can only conclude by thanking you for the kind and courteous terms in which you express your appreciation of the spirit of justice and impartiality with which my brother and I endeavoured, though unsuccessfully, to steer the ship of Industrial Partnership through troubled waters during the periods of extraordinarily rapid inflation and equally rapid depression in the coal trade. I trust better times may yet come, and that the story of our early success and subsequent disappointments may not be without its value : that thus the seed we have sown may yet bring forth fruit, though we have not been ourselves permitted to reap the harvest.

I remain, dear sir,
Yours sincerely,
ARCHIBALD BRIGGS.

Sedley Taylor, M.A.

APPENDIX OF REGULATIONS.

No. 1.

                                                                    PAGES
MAISON A. BORD. (IMMEDIATE PARTICIPATION.) 157, 158

No. 2.

COMPAGNIE D'ASSURANCES GÉNÉRALES.
   (DEFERRED PARTICIPATION.) 159–163

No. 3.

MAISON A. CHAIX ET COMPAGNIE. (MIXED
   PARTICIPATION.) 164–170

REGULATIONS

A. Bord, Manufacturer of pianofortes, 52, rue des Poissonniers, Paris.* (Immediate Participation.)

Art. 1.—From and after the 1st of April, 1865, all persons working in any manner in the house of Monsieur A. Bord, or specially for the said house, shall receive a dividend proportional to the work which they shall have done in the course of the year—such dividend to be fixed on the following bases :—

Art. 2.—On the 1st of April, 1865, there shall be drawn up a full balance-sheet showing the entire capital employed in the manufacture, sale and hire of pianofortes : on this capital interest at ten per cent. shall be annually paid as a first charge.

Art. 3.—On the other hand each *employé* or workman is to be provided with a pay-book in which shall be entered the total of his earnings according to the existing tariffs.

Art. 4.—After each annual balancing of accounts the profits shall be divided between M. Bord and the workmen ; the share of the former being proportional to the amount assigned to him as interest, and that of the latter being proportional to the sum received by them in payments for their work done.

Art. 5.—In order to be entitled to the dividend it is necessary to have worked in the house for six months and to be working there still at the time of the balancing of accounts : when this condition is not fulfilled only ordinary wages will be paid.

Art. 6.—For cases of sickness there will be a medical man attached to the house, and every sick workman will receive

---

* *Bulletin de la Participation*, 1882, pp. 64, 65.

further, if he is unmarried, two francs a day, and three francs if he has young children unable to support themselves ; if he is treated at a hospital, he will be entitled to only half the aforesaid allowance, (which will be paid in advance). One-half of these costs will be charged on the general dividend, and the other half on the individual dividend of the workman who has been ill. As to the fees of the medical man they will likewise be charged on the general dividend, or rather this outlay will be reckoned among the general expenses of the house.

REGULATIONS

*Compagnie d'Assurances Générales, 87, rue de Richelieu, Paris.**
(Deferred Participation.)

Art. 1.—The *Provident Fund*, founded as an act of pure liberality in favour of the *employés* and attendants of the four Companies of general Insurance (marine, fire, life and hail) is managed, under the authority of the Council of administration, conformably to the following regulations:—

Art. 2.—The Council determines what classes of *employés* are admitted to the benefits of the institution. The external agents of the Company, brokers, experts, even those who receive fixed salaries, and the hall-porters except the one at the head office of the Company, are not admitted to participate in them.

Employés who enter the service of the Company in the course of the year do not share in the profits of the current year. They only begin to participate for the first year which they have spent entirely in the service of the Company from the 1st of January to the 31st of December. For the purpose, however, of ultimately calculating the term of service of an *employé*, regard is had to the exact date of his entry.

Art. 3.—In conformity with the decisions of the general meetings of the Shareholders, there is paid over to the Provident Fund a sum equal to one-twentieth, or five per cent., of the net profits divided among the Shareholders, whether in dividends or in increase of the share-capital.

This assignment takes effect from the 1st of January which has preceded the distribution.

---

* *Bulletin de la Participation*, 1879, pp. 196–200.

The general meeting of the Shareholders can at any time reduce, for the future, this allocation of five per cent. if the Council of administration report that it is in their judgment excessive.

Art. 4.—An individual account is opened in the name of each participating *employé*.

The sums paid to the Provident Fund in virtue of Article 3 are distributed among the individual accounts in proportion to the salary received by each *employé* during the year ending the 31st of December, which has preceded the distribution.

Art. 5.—A bonus is added to each individual account consisting of interest at four per cent., calculated, on the 31st of December of each year, upon the sum total standing in it, except in case of earlier settlement of accounts which there is occasion to liquidate in the course of the year.

Art. 6.—The Provident Fund is common to the four Companies, in respect to the *employés*, whom it tends to make into a single family and to unite in relations of mutual assistance.

There exists, therefore, entire mutuality between the *employés* of the four Companies in regard to the distribution of sums arising from participation in profits and of sums arising from lapses, whatever be the Companies which produce the profits, or to which the *employés* lapsed from their rights belong.

Art. 7.—When an *employé* has completed his twenty-fifth year of service, or, failing that, his sixty-fifth year of age, and only if one or other of these conditions is satisfied, his claim on the Provident Fund is definitively acquired.

His individual account may be liquidated, either on his demand, or officially by decision of the Council of administration, which may order his retirement: the employment to be made of the sum arising from the liquidation of his individual account is determined in conformity with Article 15 of the present Regulations.

Art. 8.—In case of the death of an *employé* in active service leaving behind him a widow, legitimate children, adopted children, children legitimated by subsequent marriage, grandchildren or ascendant relatives, the sums placed to his credit up to the 31st of December which preceded his decease are remitted, whatever be his age and the duration of his services, in one or in several payments, to his widow, to his children or grandchildren, or to his ascendants, in the manner, at the periods, and in the proportions determined by the Council of administration.

Art. 9.—If an *employé* is attacked by infirmity recognised as involving incapacity for work, the Council may dispose in his favour of the whole or part of the sum standing in his account.

Art. 10.—If an *employé* of the Company becomes its Managing Director, his account is liquidated on the day of his appointment.

The sum total standing to his credit is put at his disposal in ready money.

Art. 11.—If an *employé* of the Company quits its participating employment in order to continue regularly serving it in an external function, as agent, broker, expert, or in any other manner, with the approval of the Council, the Council may dispose to his advantage of the whole or part of the sum standing in his account.

The Council may adjourn this grant to a later period and subject it to such conditions as it may see fit to make.

Art. 12.—In all cases of dissolution and liquidation of the Company not followed by reconstitution, and in those when *employés* are dismissed, without any motive for dissatisfaction, by a measure of reduction of staff or suppression of employment decided on in Council, the accounts of the dismissed *employés* are liquidated on the day of the cessation of their services, and the sums standing to their individual credit are placed at their disposal in ready money, whatever be the number of their years of service.

Art. 13.—Except in the above cases an *employé* who voluntarily quits, or is dismissed from, the service of the Company forfeits every claim, immediate and prospective, on the Provident Fund.

The sum standing in his individual account is distributed, on the 31st of December which follows his departure, among all the other participating accounts in proportion to the sums already standing in them.

The same distribution takes place at the death of an *employé* who leaves neither widow, descendants nor ascendants.

If, however, the retired, dismissed or deceased *employé* is in debt to the Company, the sum standing in his account is applied in the first place, and as far as it will go, to make good the deficit, or repair the injury done by him to the Company.

The Council also reserves to itself the power of estimating the degree of the misconduct of an *employé* whom it is led to dismiss, and, if there is room for the exercise of indulgence, that of handing over to him on dismissal a part of the sum standing in his individual account, without however being bound to give any reason for its decisions.

Art. 14.—The *employé* who has completed his twenty-fifth year of service, or his sixty-fifth year of age, can have his individual account settled though he still remains in the service of the Company, provided that he obtains the consent of the Council on this point.

In this case, his account ceases to benefit by lapses, but goes on being increased by interest and by participation in profits, without, however, any payment being made to the *employé* until he quits the service of the Company.

Art. 15.—When there is occasion to liquidate the account of an *employé* who has completed his twenty-fifth year of service, or his sixty-fifth year of age, the *employé* may require that the sum disposable be applied, either to settle upon him a life annuity in the *Company of general life insurances*, with or without reversion to his widow or to any other person approved by the Council, all in accordance with the tariffs in force at the time of the settlement, or to purchase for him French State Funds or registered shares in French railways, the share-certificates remaining deposited in the Company's office until the death of the beneficiary, to be then remitted to the recipients by him testamentarily designated.

The Council alone is judge of the exceptional circumstances under which it may consent to make a different employment of the disposable sum, or even to hand it over in ready money; it is not bound to give any reason for its decisions.

Art. 16.—Every *employé* whose account is liquidated, except in the cases provided for by Article 12, gives his word of honour in writing not to carry his services to any other Insurance office without the Company's express written authorisation.

If he fails to fulfil this engagement, all sums and all arrears received by him arising from the liquidation of his account may be reclaimed for the benefit of the Provident Fund.

All sums remaining deposited in his name, all securities, all policies of life annuity, etc., may also, if the Council so directs, revert to the Provident Fund.

Art. 17.—The distribution among the several individual accounts of lapsed sums due to death, withdrawal or dismissal takes place only once a year, on the 31st of December.

The assignment of five per cent. on the profits is likewise always reputed as made on the 31st of December, although the actual payment can only be made later, after the approval of the accounts by the general Meeting.

In consequence the individual accounts which have to be liquidated in the course of the year are always settled on the preceding 31st of December, except as to calculation of interest up to the day of liquidation, and they neither share in the eventual profits of the current year nor derive any benefit from changes in the staff of *employés* during that year.

Art. 18.—The *employés* of the Company can put forward no claim whatever to the sums carried to their individual accounts, except by having fulfilled the conditions established by the present regulations.

The Council may modify the present regulations provided that no retrospective effect be produced by such modification.

The Council expressly reserves to itself the plenitude of its action and of its authority over the *employés* of the Company, in conformity with the statutes, especially in regard to dismissals of which it remains absolute arbiter, without being bound under any circumstances to state reasons for its decisions.

Art. 19.—In all cases, the sums to be paid, the interests or life annuities to be supplied by virtue of the present enactments, whether to *employés* of the Company, to their widows, heirs or other designated persons, are beforehand expressly declared to be granted on the score of liberality and as alimony, and as such to be incapable of cession or seizure.

This declaration is to be reproduced on all registers, accounts and deeds where occasion may require.

Art. 20.—The final decision on complaints or claims of any kind in reference to the provisions of the present regulations lies with the Council of administration, which remains their sole and sovereign judge without right of challenge or appeal.

REGULATIONS

A. Chaix et Compagnie, railway printers publishers and booksellers, 20, *rue Bergère, Paris.** (Mixed Participation.)

Art. 1.—From and after the 1st of January, 1872, an interest consisting in a share of the net profits of the year will be allotted gratuitously to all the *employés* or workpeople of both sexes who shall have been designated as participants in these advantages.

This share is fixed for the year 1872 at ten per cent.

Art. 2.—To be admitted as participants, the workmen, workwomen and *employés* must have three years of consecutive presence in the House, must have made proof of zeal and aptitude in their functions, and must address to M. Chaix an application accompanied by a certificate of birth.

In order to form the first participating body, all those are from this day forward admitted who, on the 1st of January, 1872, have had at least three years of consecutive presence in the House.

Art. 3.—Beyond the body of participants, *candidates for participation* may, according to their services, be called to enjoy a part of the advantages of participation. A decision of the Consulting Committee will fix each year the nature and extent of these advantages.

Art. 4.—The apprentices of the House will be admitted as participants from and after the 1st of January preceding the close of their apprenticeship; but their twenty years of presence will only be reckoned from the date of their majority.

---

* *Bulletin de la Participation,* 1879, pp. 116-122.

Art. 5.—The distribution of the share in profits among the participants will be made in proportion to the sums which they shall have received during the year, whether in salaries or in wages, and according to the arrangements fixed in Article 6 here following.

In determining the dividend of each individual no account will be taken of gratuities or of other variable allowances.

Art. 6.—The sum allotted to each participant will be divided into two equal parts :

One of these will be paid over to him every year, after the approval of the balance-sheet, and at fixed epochs : the other will be placed to his Provident and Pension account which is referred to below.

Art. 7.—Every participant who shall voluntarily have quitted the House before the end of the year, will lose all right to the participation of the current year.

Art. 8.—A participant who is dismissed will not, whatever be the reason for his dismissal, lose his rights in the participation ; his interest in profits will, however, end with the month preceding that in which he quits the House.

Art. 9.—In the two cases provided for in Articles 7 and 8 the participant cannot claim the first part of the sum allotted to him in virtue of Article 6 before the time of the general distribution, and he will receive it under the same conditions as the other participants.

The second part will be liquidated in accordance with Articles 19 and 23.

Art. 10.—In the event of decrease in business, or of a temporary withdrawal from the House, due to whatever cause, the participant who wishes to preserve his rights must obtain *beforehand* from M. Chaix written leave of absence.

Art. 11.—Participants who have quitted the House under the conditions contemplated by Article 10 must hold themselves in readiness to obey the summons which will be addressed to them. Should they fail to appear, a notice will be sent to their residence by registered letter to which they shall be held bound to reply within forty-eight hours at the latest, engaging to return to the House in the course of eight days, failing which they shall be reputed to have resigned at the date of their withdrawal from the House.

Art. 12.—Participants obliged to quit the House in order to perform their military service, and who wish to preserve their rights, are to inform M. Chaix of the fact. They are further required to apply to him, in the month succeeding the expiration of their term of military duty, for readmission to their employment.

Provident and Pension Fund.

Art. 13.—The Provident and Pension Fund is established for the benefit of the workmen, workwomen and *employés* of the House who are participants.

Art. 14.—In order to have a right to all the advantages conferred by this Fund, it is necessary to have worked continuously for the House during at least twenty years, or to have reached the age of sixty years.

In calculating the period of service, account will be taken of years of uninterrupted presence anterior to the 1st of January, 1872.

Periods of absence contemplated by Articles 10 and 12 are to be replaced by equivalent periods of presence.

Art. 15.—The Provident and Pension Fund is formed by means of payments made to the account of each beneficiary agreeably to paragraph 3 of Article 6.

Art. 16.—Further, an additional sum, taken from the profits of the House and fixed each year by M. Chaix, will be paid to the account of each participant in proportion to the total of that account.

This sum will for 1872 be five per cent. on the year's profits.

The accumulations hence resulting will, however, only accrue to the participants provided they have fulfilled the conditions of age or of service stated in Article 14.

Art. 16 (*bis*).—In no case can the total share annually allotted to each participant in virtue of Articles 6 and 16 exceed one-fourth of his salary or wages.

The surplus, if there be any, will be distributed, without distinction of services, among the participants having ten complete years of presence, and in proportion to their years of service.

This supplementary share will not, however, accrue to these

participants unless they satisfy the conditions of age or of standing laid down in Article 14.

Art. 17.—When a participant, having completed his twentieth year of service or, failing that, his sixtieth year of age, quits the House voluntarily or in consequence of dismissal, his Provident and Pension account is liquidated on his demand, in accordance with Article 23.

Art. 18.—The participant who has completed his twentieth year of service or his sixtieth year of age may also, though continuing in the employ of the House, require the liquidation of his Provident and Pension account in accordance with Article 23.

In this case his account ceases to share in the advantages resulting from lapses; but it continues to accumulate by participation and by the payments made by M. Chaix in virtue of Article 16, but the liquidation of this new account cannot take place until its owner quits the House.

Art. 19.—Every participant who, before having attained his twentieth year of presence or his sixtieth year of age, quits the House, either voluntarily or in consequence of dismissal, may require the liquidation of his Provident and Pension account ; but this liquidation must, *on pain of forfeiture*, be demanded in writing of M. Chaix within the period of one year and one day from the date of the participant's departure. This liquidation includes only the sums paid under Article 6 ; it takes place under the conditions provided in Article 23 and not until one year after the participant has left the House.

The sums paid to his account in accordance with Article 16 are distributed among the accounts of the remaining participants in proportion to the sums already standing in them respectively.

Art. 20.—When a participant dies in active service, the sums placed in his account conformably to Articles 6 and 16 are handed over to the members of his family designated in Article 24, in one or several payments, in the manner, at the times and in the proportions determined by the Committee.

Art. 21.—If a participant is attacked by infirmity recognised as involving incapacity for work, the whole or a part of the sums placed in his account under Article 6 may, after consultation of the Committee, be handed over to him at once.

Art. 22.—If a participant who leaves the House either voluntarily or by dismissal or death, is in its debt, the sum standing in his account is, in the first place, employed, as far as it will go, to supply the deficit, or to repair the damage which he has caused to the House.

Should this deficit or damage arise from embezzlements committed by the participant, he would incur the forfeiture of his rights and the House would resume possession of the sum standing in his name.

Art. 23.—On the liquidation of the individual account of a participant, he may at his choice require that the disposable sum be applied to purchase for him a life annuity in the State Pension Office, (*Caisse des Retraites de e'État*) or in a Life Insurance Company, with or without reversion to the members of his family appointed by the present regulations to succeed to the enjoyment of it,—or to purchase for him French Government securities or shares in French railways, or lastly the interests arising from such securities or shares—the certificates remaining in the office of the House, or in an assigned office of deposit, up to the death of the titulary, in order to be handed over to the members of his family designated in the following Article.

Art. 24.—The persons appointed to receive, after the death of a participant, the sums placed in his account are :—

1. Wife or husband where no legal separation has occurred.
2. Children, legitimate or legitimated by subsequent marriage, adopted children and grandchildren.
3. Ascendant relatives.

The Committee of consultation may, on the demand of the persons interested, modify the above provision.

Failing the successors above appointed, the sums or securities arising from the liquidation of a deceased participant's account are placed to the credit of the remaining participants in proportion to the sums already standing in their respective accounts.

Art. 25.—The distribution of lapsed sums among the different individual accounts takes place but once a year, on the 31st of December and exclusively for the benefit of the members present in the House at that time.

The allotment of the share in profits is likewise made once

a year after approval of the accounts and balance-sheet by the general Meeting of the sleeping partners of the House.

In consequence, the individual accounts which have to be liquidated in the course of the year are always made up on the preceding 31st of December.

Art. 26.—The account of each participant will be credited with a yearly interest of four per cent. produced by the sums standing in it, so long as the House retains the financial management of these sums.

This management may, with the assent of the Consulting Committee, be eventually entrusted either to an insurance company, a society of credit or a public department.

Consulting Committee of Superintendence.

Art. 27.—A Consulting Committee of Superintendence is instituted to assist M. Chaix in carrying out the provisions relating to profit-sharing and to the Provident and Pension Fund.

Art. 28.—This Committee is composed of nineteen members, viz. M. Chaix — the nine office-bearers of the Mutual Aid Society,* renewed each year three at a time in general Meeting —the three senior heads of department and foremen—and the six senior workmen, workwomen or *employés* of the House.

Art. 29.—The ordinary meetings of the Committee take place once every three weeks. Extraordinary meetings are specially summoned.

General Provisions.

Art. 30.—There shall be delivered to every participant a pass-book in which shall be entered all the sums placed to his account.

Art. 31.—As the title of participant implies special conditions of stability and attachment to the establishment, no participant can be definitively dismissed without a decision of M. Chaix.

Art. 32.—The sums to be paid, the dividends interests or

---

* This is an independent Society supported by a drawback on wages, membership in which is obligatory on every person employed by the House.

pensions to be supplied, in consequence of the present regulations, whether to participants or to the members of their families designated in Article 24, are beforehand expressly declared to be free gifts and for alimony and, as such, incapable of cession or seizure.

Art. 33.—It is declared that M. Chaix is sole judge of all claims which may arise in reference to the present regulations. He will, however, hear the opinion of the Consulting Committee.

Art. 34.—The yearly division of profits takes place after the approval of the accounts by the sleeping partners of the House, but the participants do not possess the right of intermeddling in any respect with the book-keeping.

Art. 35.—*Employés*, workmen and workwomen coming from an establishment provided with similar institutions and in which they are already participating members will, on their demand, be admitted *ipso facto* as *candidates for participation*. The length of their period of probation for becoming participants will be fixed by the Committee within the three months following their admission to the House, but is in no case to exceed one year.

Art. 36.—The present provisions apply to the *employés* of the bookselling department, in so far as concerns the profits realised in that branch.

Art. 37.—Modifications which experience may render it advisable to make in the present regulations shall produce no retrospective effect.

Art. 38.—M. Chaix expressly reserves to himself the power of abolishing the present regulations in the event of his not being satisfied with their results.

Should that step be determined upon, the Provident Fund would be liquidated on the next following 31st of December, and the sums or securities appertaining to it would be individually distributed as cash, after approval by the sleeping partners of the House of the year's balance-sheet.

Art. 39.—If at M. Chaix's death his successors did not choose to continue profit-sharing, the Provident and Pension Fund would be liquidated as directed in the preceding Article.

PRINTED BY WILLIAM CLOWES AND SONS, LIMITED, LONDON AND BECCLES.

A LIST OF

KEGAN PAUL, TRENCH & CO.'S

PUBLICATIONS.

10.83.

1, *Paternoster Square,*
London.

A LIST OF
KEGAN PAUL, TRENCH & CO.'S PUBLICATIONS.

CONTENTS.

	PAGE		PAGE
GENERAL LITERATURE.	2	POETRY.	30
INTERNATIONAL SCIENTIFIC SERIES	26	WORKS OF FICTION	37
		BOOKS FOR THE YOUNG	38
MILITARY WORKS.	29		

GENERAL LITERATURE.

ADAMSON, H. T., B.D.—**The Truth as it is in Jesus.** Crown 8vo, 8s. 6d.

The Three Sevens. Crown 8vo, 5s. 6d.

The Millennium; or, the Mystery of God Finished. Crown 8vo, 6s.

A. K. H. B.—**From a Quiet Place.** A New Volume of Sermons. Crown 8vo, 5s.

ALLEN, Rev. R., M.A.—**Abraham: his Life, Times, and Travels,** 3800 years ago. With Map. Second Edition. Post 8vo, 6s.

ALLIES, T. W., M.A.—**Per Crucem ad Lucem.** The Result of a Life. 2 vols. Demy 8vo, 25s.

A Life's Decision. Crown 8vo, 7s. 6d.

AMOS, Professor Sheldon.—**The History and Principles of the Civil Law of Rome.** An aid to the Study of Scientific and Comparative Jurisprudence. Demy 8vo. 16s.

ANDERDON, Rev. W. H.—**Fasti Apostolici;** a Chronology of the Years between the Ascension of our Lord and the Martyrdom of SS. Peter and Paul. Second Edition. Crown 8vo, 2s. 6d.

Evenings with the Saints. Crown 8vo, 5s.

ARMSTRONG, Richard A., B.A.—**Latter-Day Teachers.** Six Lectures. Small crown 8vo, 2s. 6d.

AUBERTIN, J. J.—**A Flight to Mexico.** With Seven full-page Illustrations and a Railway Map of Mexico. Crown 8vo, 7s. 6d.

BADGER, George Percy, D.C.L.—**An English-Arabic Lexicon.** In which the equivalent for English Words and Idiomatic Sentences are rendered into literary and colloquial Arabic. Royal 4to, £9 9s.

BAGEHOT, Walter.—**The English Constitution.** Third Edition. Crown 8vo, 7s. 6d.

Lombard Street. A Description of the Money Market. Eighth Edition. Crown 8vo, 7s. 6d.

Some Articles on the Depreciation of Silver, and Topics connected with it. Demy 8vo, 5s.

BAGENAL, Philip H.—**The American-Irish and their Influence on Irish Politics.** Crown 8vo, 5s.

BAGOT, Alan, C.E.—**Accidents in Mines:** their Causes and Prevention. Crown 8vo, 6s.

The Principles of Colliery Ventilation. Second Edition, greatly enlarged. Crown 8vo, 5s.

BAKER, Sir Sherston, Bart.—**The Laws relating to Quarantine.** Crown 8vo, 12s. 6d.

BALDWIN, Capt. J. H.—**The Large and Small Game of Bengal and the North-Western Provinces of India.** With 18 Illustrations. New and Cheaper Edition. Small 4to, 10s. 6d.

BALLIN, Ada S. and F. L.—**A Hebrew Grammar.** With Exercises selected from the Bible. Crown 8vo, 7s. 6d.

BARCLAY, Edgar.—**Mountain Life in Algeria.** With numerous Illustrations by Photogravure. Crown 4to, 16s.

BARLOW, James H.—**The Ultimatum of Pessimism.** An Ethical Study. Demy 8vo, 6s.

BARNES, William.—**Outlines of Redecraft (Logic).** With English Wording. Crown 8vo, 3s.

BAUR, Ferdinand, Dr. Ph.—**A Philological Introduction to Greek and Latin for Students.** Translated and adapted from the German, by C. KEGAN PAUL, M.A., and E. D. STONE, M.A. Third Edition. Crown 8vo, 6s.

BELLARS, Rev. W.—**The Testimony of Conscience to the Truth and Divine Origin of the Christian Revelation.** Burney Prize Essay. Small crown 8vo, 3s. 6d.

BELLINGHAM, Henry, M.P.—**Social Aspects of Catholicism and Protestantism in their Civil Bearing upon Nations.** Translated and adapted from the French of M. le BARON DE HAULLEVILLE. With a preface by His Eminence CARDINAL MANNING. Second and Cheaper Edition. Crown 8vo, 3s. 6d.

BELLINGHAM H. Belsches Graham.—Ups and Downs of Spanish Travel. Second Edition. Crown 8vo. 5s.

BENN, Alfred W.—The Greek Philosophers. 2 vols. Demy 8vo, 28s.

BENT, J. Theodore.—Genoa: How the Republic Rose and Fell. With 18 Illustrations. Demy 8vo, 18s.

BLOOMFIELD, The Lady.—Reminiscences of Court and Diplomatic Life. New and Cheaper Edition. With Frontispiece. Crown 8vo, 6s.

BLUNT, The Ven. Archdeacon.—The Divine Patriot, and other Sermons. Preached in Scarborough and in Cannes. New and Cheaper Edition. Crown 8vo, 4s. 6d.

BLUNT, Wilfred S.—The Future of Islam. Crown 8vo, 6s.

BONWICK, J., F.R.G.S.—Pyramid Facts and Fancies. Crown 8vo, 5s.

BOUVERIE-PUSEY, S. E. B.—Permanence and Evolution. An Inquiry into the Supposed Mutability of Animal Types. Crown 8vo, 5s.

BOWEN, H. C., M.A.—Studies in English. For the use of Modern Schools. Third Edition. Small crown 8vo, 1s. 6d.

English Grammar for Beginners. Fcap. 8vo, 1s.

BRADLEY, F. H.—The Principles of Logic. Demy 8vo, 16s.

BRIDGETT, Rev. T. E.—History of the Holy Eucharist in Great Britain. 2 vols. Demy 8vo, 18s.

BRODRICK, the Hon. G. C.—Political Studies. Demy 8vo, 14s.

BROOKE, Rev. S. A.—Life and Letters of the Late Rev. F. W. Robertson, M.A. Edited by.

    I. Uniform with Robertson's Sermons. 2 vols. With Steel Portrait. 7s. 6d.
    II. Library Edition. With Portrait. 8vo, 12s.
    III. A Popular Edition. In 1 vol., 8vo, 6s.

The Fight of Faith. Sermons preached on various occasions. Fifth Edition. Crown 8vo, 7s. 6d.

The Spirit of the Christian Life. New and Cheaper Edition. Crown 8vo, 5s.

Theology in the English Poets.—Cowper, Coleridge, Wordsworth, and Burns. Fifth and Cheaper Edition. Post 8vo, 5s.

Christ in Modern Life. Sixteenth and Cheaper Edition. Crown 8vo, 5s.

Sermons. First Series. Thirteenth and Cheaper Edition. Crown 8vo, 5s.

Sermons. Second Series. Sixth and Cheaper Edition. Crown 8vo, 5s.

BROWN, *Rev. J. Baldwin, B.A.*—**The Higher Life.** Its Reality, Experience, and Destiny. Fifth Edition. Crown 8vo, 5s.

Doctrine of Annihilation in the Light of the Gospel of Love. Five Discourses. Fourth Edition. Crown 8vo, 2s. 6d.

The Christian Policy of Life. A Book for Young Men of Business. Third Edition. Crown 8vo, 3s. 6d.

BROWN, *S. Borton, B.A.*—**The Fire Baptism of all Flesh;** or, the Coming Spiritual Crisis of the Dispensation. Crown 8vo, 6s.

BROWNBILL, *John.*—**Principles of English Canon Law.** Part I. General Introduction. Crown 8vo, 6s.

BROWNE, *W. R.*—**The Inspiration of the New Testament.** With a Preface by the Rev. J. P. NORRIS, D.D. Fcap. 8vo, 2s. 6d.

BURTON, *Mrs. Richard.*—**The Inner Life of Syria, Palestine, and the Holy Land.** Cheaper Edition in one volume. Large post 8vo. 7s. 6d.

BUSBECQ, *Ogier Ghiselin de.*—**His Life and Letters.** By CHARLES THORNTON FORSTER, M.A., and F. H. BLACKBURNE DANIELL, M.A. 2 vols. With Frontispieces. Demy 8vo, 24s.

CARPENTER, *W. B., LL.D., M.D., F.R.S., etc.*—**The Principles of Mental Physiology.** With their Applications to the Training and Discipline of the Mind, and the Study of its Morbid Conditions. Illustrated. Sixth Edition. 8vo, 12s.

CERVANTES.—**The Ingenious Knight Don Quixote de la Mancha.** A New Translation from the Originals of 1605 and 1608. By A. J. DUFFIELD. With Notes. 3 vols. Demy 8vo, 42s.

Journey to Parnassus. Spanish Text, with Translation into English Tercets, Preface, and Illustrative Notes, by JAMES Y. GIBSON. Crown 8vo, 12s.

CHEYNE, *Rev. T. K.*—**The Prophecies of Isaiah.** Translated with Critical Notes and Dissertations. 2 vols. Second Edition. Demy 8vo, 25s.

CLAIRAUT.—**Elements of Geometry.** Translated by Dr. KAINES. With 145 Figures. Crown 8vo, 4s. 6d.

CLAYDEN, *P. W.*—**England under Lord Beaconsfield.** The Political History of the Last Six Years, from the end of 1873 to the beginning of 1880. Second Edition, with Index and continuation to March, 1880. Demy 8vo, 16s.

Samuel Sharpe. Egyptologist and Translator of the Bible. Crown 8vo, 6s.

CLIFFORD, *Samuel.*—**What Think Ye of Christ?** Crown 8vo. 6s.

CLODD, *Edward, F.R.A.S.*—**The Childhood of the World:** a Simple Account of Man in Early Times. Seventh Edition. Crown 8vo, 3s.

A Special Edition for Schools. 1s.

CLODD, *Edward, F.R.A.S.—continued.*

    The Childhood of Religions. Including a Simple Account of the Birth and Growth of Myths and Legends. Eighth Thousand. Crown 8vo, 5s.

        A Special Edition for Schools. 1s. 6d.

    Jesus of Nazareth. With a brief sketch of Jewish History to the Time of His Birth. Small crown 8vo, 6s.

COGHLAN, *J. Cole, D.D.*—**The Modern Pharisee and other Sermons.** Edited by the Very Rev. H. H. DICKINSON, D.D., Dean of Chapel Royal, Dublin. New and Cheaper Edition. Crown 8vo, 7s. 6d.

COLERIDGE, *Sara.*—**Memoir and Letters of Sara Coleridge.** Edited by her Daughter. With Index. Cheap Edition. With Portrait. 7s. 6d.

Collects Exemplified. Being Illustrations from the Old and New Testaments of the Collects for the Sundays after Trinity. By the Author of "A Commentary on the Epistles and Gospels." Edited by the Rev. JOSEPH JACKSON. Crown 8vo, 5s.

CONNELL, *A. K.*—**Discontent and Danger in India.** Small crown 8vo, 3s. 6d.

    The Economic Revolution of India. Crown 8vo, 5s.

CORY, *William.*—**A Guide to Modern English History.** Part I.—MDCCCXV.-MDCCCXXX. Demy 8vo, 9s. Part II.—MDCCCXXX.-MDCCCXXXV., 15s.

COTTERILL, *H. B.*—**An Introduction to the Study of Poetry.** Crown 8vo, 7s. 6d.

COX, *Rev. Sir George W., M.A., Bart.*—**A History of Greece from the Earliest Period to the end of the Persian War.** New Edition. 2 vols. Demy 8vo, 36s.

    The Mythology of the Aryan Nations. New Edition. Demy 8vo, 16s.

    Tales of Ancient Greece. New Edition. Small crown 8vo, 6s.

    A Manual of Mythology in the form of Question and Answer. New Edition. Fcap. 8vo, 3s.

    An Introduction to the Science of Comparative Mythology and Folk-Lore. Second Edition. Crown 8vo. 7s. 6d.

COX, *Rev. Sir G. W., M.A., Bart., and JONES, Eustace Hinton.*—**Popular Romances of the Middle Ages.** Second Edition, in 1 vol. Crown 8vo, 6s.

COX, *Rev. Samuel, D.D.*—**Salvator Mundi ; or, Is Christ the Saviour of all Men?** Eighth Edition. Crown 8vo, 5s.

    The Genesis of Evil, and other Sermons, mainly expository. Third Edition. Crown 8vo, 6s.

COX, *Rev. Samuel, D.D.—continued.*
A Commentary on the Book of Job. With a Translation. Demy 8vo, 15*s*.
The Larger Hope. A Sequel to "Salvator Mundi." 16mo, 1*s*.

CRAVEN, *Mrs.*—A Year's Meditations. Crown 8vo, 6*s*.

CRAWFURD, *Oswald.*—Portugal, Old and New. With Illustrations and Maps. New and Cheaper Edition. Crown 8vo, 6*s*.

CROZIER, *John Beattie, M.B.*—The Religion of the Future. Crown 8vo, 6*s*.

Cyclopædia of Common Things. Edited by the Rev. Sir GEORGE W. Cox, Bart., M.A. With 500 Illustrations. Third Edition. Large post 8vo, 7*s*. 6*d*.

DAVIDSON, *Rev. Samuel, D.D., LL.D.*—Canon of the Bible: Its Formation, History, and Fluctuations. Third and Revised Edition. Small crown 8vo, 5*s*.
The Doctrine of Last Things contained in the New Testament compared with the Notions of the Jews and the Statements of Church Creeds. Small crown 8vo, 3*s*. 6*d*.

DAVIDSON, *Thomas.*—The Parthenon Frieze, and other Essays. Crown 8vo, 6*s*.

DAWSON, *Geo., M.A.* Prayers, with a Discourse on Prayer. Edited by his Wife. Eighth Edition. Crown 8vo, 6*s*.
Sermons on Disputed Points and Special Occasions. Edited by his Wife. Fourth Edition. Crown 8vo, 6*s*.
Sermons on Daily Life and Duty. Edited by his Wife. Fourth Edition. Crown 8vo, 6*s*.
The Authentic Gospel. A New Volume of Sermons. Edited by GEORGE ST. CLAIR. Third Edition. Crown 8vo, 6*s*.
Three Books of God: Nature, History, and Scripture. Sermons edited by GEORGE ST. CLAIR. Crown 8vo, 6*s*.

DE JONCOURT, *Madame Marie.*—Wholesome Cookery. Crown 8vo, 3*s*. 6*d*.

DE LONG, *Lieut. Com. G. W.*—The Voyage of the Jeannette. The Ship and Ice Journals of. Edited by his Wife, EMMA DE LONG. With Portraits, Maps, and many Illustrations on wood and stone. 2 vols. Demy 8vo. 36*s*.

DESPREZ, *Phillip S., B.D.*—Daniel and John ; or, the Apocalypse of the Old and that of the New Testament. Demy 8vo, 12*s*.

DOWDEN, *Edward, LL.D.*—Shakspere: a Critical Study of his Mind and Art. Sixth Edition. Post 8vo, 12*s*.
Studies in Literature, 1789-1877. Second and Cheaper Edition. Large post 8vo, 6*s*.

DUFFIELD, A. J.—**Don Quixote: his Critics and Commentators.** With a brief account of the minor works of MIGUEL DE CERVANTES SAAVEDRA, and a statement of the aim and end of the greatest of them all. A handy book for general readers. Crown 8vo, 3s. 6d.

DU MONCEL, Count.—**The Telephone, the Microphone, and the Phonograph.** With 74 Illustrations. Second Edition. Small crown 8vo, 5s.

EDGEWORTH, F. Y.—**Mathematical Psychics.** An Essay on the Application of Mathematics to Social Science. Demy 8vo, 7s. 6d.

Educational Code of the Prussian Nation, in its Present Form. In accordance with the Decisions of the Common Provincial Law, and with those of Recent Legislation. Crown 8vo, 2s. 6d.

Education Library. Edited by PHILIP MAGNUS:—

    An Introduction to the History of Educational Theories. By OSCAR BROWNING, M.A. Second Edition. 3s. 6d.

    Old Greek Education. By the Rev. Prof. MAHAFFY, M.A. 3s. 6d.

    School Management. Including a general view of the work of Education, Organization and Discipline. By JOSEPH LANDON. Second Edition. 6s.

Eighteenth Century Essays. Selected and Edited by AUSTIN DOBSON. With a Miniature Frontispiece by R. Caldecott. Parchment Library Edition, 6s.; vellum, 7s. 6d.

ELSDALE, Henry.—**Studies in Tennyson's Idylls.** Crown 8vo, 5s.

ELYOT, Sir Thomas.—**The Boke named the Gouernour.** Edited from the First Edition of 1531 by HENRY HERBERT STEPHEN CROFT, M.A., Barrister-at-Law. With Portraits of Sir Thomas and Lady Elyot, copied by permission of her Majesty from Holbein's Original Drawings at Windsor Castle. 2 vols. Fcap. 4to, 50s.

Enoch the Prophet. The Book of. Archbishop LAURENCE'S Translation, with an Introduction by the Author of "The Evolution of Christianity." Crown 8vo, 5s.

Eranus. A Collection of Exercises in the Alcaic and Sapphic Metres. Edited by F. W. CORNISH, Assistant Master at Eton. Crown 8vo, 2s.

EVANS, Mark.—**The Story of Our Father's Love,** told to Children. Sixth and Cheaper Edition. With Four Illustrations. Fcap. 8vo, 1s. 6d.

EVANS, Mark—continued.
A Book of Common Prayer and Worship for Household Use, compiled exclusively from the Holy Scriptures. Second Edition. Fcap. 8vo, 1s.

The Gospel of Home Life. Crown 8vo, 4s. 6d.

The King's Story-Book. In Three Parts. Fcap. 8vo, 1s. 6d. each.

*** Parts I. and II. with Eight Illustrations and Two Picture Maps, now ready.

"Fan Kwae" at Canton before Treaty Days 1825-1844. By an old Resident. With Frontispiece. Crown 8vo, 5s.

FLECKER, Rev. Eliezer.—Scripture Onomatology. Being Critical Notes on the Septuagint and other versions. Crown 8vo, 3s. 6d.

FLOREDICE, W. H.—A Month among the Mere Irish. Small crown 8vo, 5s.

GARDINER, Samuel R., and J. BASS MULLINGER, M.A.—Introduction to the Study of English History. Large Crown 8vo, 9s.

GARDNER, Dorsey.—Quatre Bras, Ligny, and Waterloo. A Narrative of the Campaign in Belgium, 1815. With Maps and Plans. Demy 8vo, 16s.

Genesis in Advance of Present Science. A Critical Investigation of Chapters I.-IX. By a Septuagenarian Beneficed Presbyter. Demy 8vo. 10s. 6d.

GENNA, E.—Irresponsible Philanthropists. Being some Chapters on the Employment of Gentlewomen. Small crown 8vo, 2s. 6d.

GEORGE, Henry.—Progress and Poverty : An Inquiry into the Causes of Industrial Depressions, and of Increase of Want with Increase of Wealth. The Remedy. Second Edition. Post 8vo, 7s. 6d. Also a Cheap Edition. Limp cloth, 1s. 6d. Paper covers, 1s.

GIBSON, James Y.—Journey to Parnassus. Composed by MIGUEL DE CERVANTES SAAVEDRA. Spanish Text, with Translation into English Tercets, Preface, and Illustrative Notes, by. Crown 8vo, 12s.

Glossary of Terms and Phrases. Edited by the Rev. H. PERCY SMITH and others. Medium 8vo, 12s.

GLOVER, F., M.A.—Exempla Latina. A First Construing Book, with Short Notes, Lexicon, and an Introduction to the Analysis of Sentences. Fcap. 8vo, 2s.

GOLDSMID, Sir Francis Henry, Bart., Q.C., M.P.—Memoir of. With Portrait. Second Edition, Revised. Crown 8vo, 6s.

GOODENOUGH, *Commodore J. G.*—Memoir of, with Extracts from his Letters and Journals. Edited by his Widow. With Steel Engraved Portrait. Square 8vo, 5s.

⁎ Also a Library Edition with Maps, Woodcuts, and Steel Engraved Portrait. Square post 8vo, 14s.

GOSSE, *Edmund W.*—Studies in the Literature of Northern Europe. With a Frontispiece designed and etched by Alma Tadema. New and Cheaper Edition. Large crown 8vo, 6s.

Seventeenth Century Studies. A Contribution to the History of English Poetry. Demy 8vo, 10s. 6d.

GOULD, *Rev. S. Baring, M.A.*—Germany, Present and Past. New and Cheaper Edition. Large crown 8vo, 7s. 6d.

GOWAN, *Major Walter E.*—A. Ivanoff's Russian Grammar. (16th Edition.) Translated, enlarged, and arranged for use of Students of the Russian Language. Demy 8vo, 6s.

GOWER, *Lord Ronald.* My Reminiscences. Second Edition. 2 vols. With Frontispieces. Demy 8vo, 30s.

GRAHAM, *William, M.A.*—The Creed of Science, Religious, Moral, and Social. Demy 8vo, 6s.

GRIFFITH, *Thomas, A.M.*—The Gospel of the Divine Life: a Study of the Fourth Evangelist. Demy 8vo, 14s.

GRIMLEY, *Rev. H. N., M.A.*—Tremadoc Sermons, chiefly on the Spiritual Body, the Unseen World, and the Divine Humanity. Third Edition. Crown 8vo, 6s.

HAECKEL, *Prof. Ernst.*—The History of Creation. Translation revised by Professor E. RAY LANKESTER, M.A., F.R.S. With Coloured Plates and Genealogical Trees of the various groups of both Plants and Animals. 2 vols. Third Edition. Post 8vo, 32s.

The History of the Evolution of Man. With numerous Illustrations. 2 vols. Post 8vo, 32s.

A Visit to Ceylon. Post 8vo, 7s. 6d.

Freedom in Science and Teaching. With a Prefatory Note by T. H. HUXLEY, F.R.S. Crown 8vo, 5s.

HALF-CROWN SERIES :—

A Lost Love. By ANNA C. OGLE [Ashford Owen].

Sister Dora : a Biography. By MARGARET LONSDALE.

True Words for Brave Men : a Book for Soldiers and Sailors. By the late CHARLES KINGSLEY.

An Inland Voyage. By R. L. STEVENSON.

Travels with a Donkey. By R. L. STEVENSON.

HALF-CROWN SERIES—*continued.*

    Notes of Travel: being Extracts from the Journals of Count VON MOLTKE.

    English Sonnets. Collected and Arranged by J. DENNIS.

    London Lyrics. By F. LOCKER.

    Home Songs for Quiet Hours. By the Rev. Canon R. H. BAYNES.

HAWEIS, Rev. H. R., M.A.—**Current Coin.** Materialism—The Devil—Crime—Drunkenness—Pauperism—Emotion—Recreation—The Sabbath. Fifth and Cheaper Edition. Crown 8vo, 5*s.*

    Arrows in the Air. Fifth and Cheaper Edition. Crown 8vo, 5*s.*

    Speech in Season. Fifth and Cheaper Edition. Crown 8vo, 5*s.*

    Thoughts for the Times. Thirteenth and Cheaper Edition. Crown 8vo, 5*s.*

    Unsectarian Family Prayers. New and Cheaper Edition. Fcap. 8vo, 1*s.* 6*d.*

HAWKINS, Edwards Comerford.—**Spirit and Form.** Sermons preached in the Parish Church of Leatherhead. Crown 8vo, 6*s.*

HAWTHORNE, Nathaniel.—**Works.** Complete in Twelve Volumes. Large post 8vo, 7*s.* 6*d.* each volume.

    VOL. I. TWICE-TOLD TALES.
        II. MOSSES FROM AN OLD MANSE.
       III. THE HOUSE OF THE SEVEN GABLES, AND THE SNOW IMAGE.
       IV. THE WONDERBOOK, TANGLEWOOD TALES, AND GRANDFATHER'S CHAIR.
       V. THE SCARLET LETTER, AND THE BLITHEDALE ROMANCE.
      VI. THE MARBLE FAUN. [Transformation.]
    VII. } OUR OLD HOME, AND ENGLISH NOTE-BOOKS.
   VIII. }
      IX. AMERICAN NOTE-BOOKS.
       X. FRENCH AND ITALIAN NOTE-BOOKS.
      XI. SEPTIMIUS FELTON, THE DOLLIVER ROMANCE, FANSHAWE, AND, IN AN APPENDIX, THE ANCESTRAL FOOTSTEP.
     XII. TALES AND ESSAYS, AND OTHER PAPERS, WITH A BIOGRAPHICAL SKETCH OF HAWTHORNE.

HAYES, A. H., Junr.—**New Colorado, and the Santa Fé Trail.** With Map and 60 Illustrations. Crown 8vo, 9*s.*

HENNESSY, Sir John Pope.—**Ralegh in Ireland.** With his Letters on Irish Affairs and some Contemporary Documents. Large crown 8vo, printed on hand-made paper, parchment, 10*s.* 6*d.*

HENRY, Philip.—**Diaries and Letters of.** Edited by MATTHEW HENRY LEE, M.A. Large crown 8vo, 7*s.* 6*d.*

HIDE, Albert.—**The Age to Come.** Small crown 8vo, 2*s.* 6*d.*

HIME, Major H. W. L., R.A.—Wagnerism: A Protest. Crown 8vo, 2s. 6d.

HINTON, J.—Life and Letters. Edited by ELLICE HOPKINS, with an Introduction by Sir W. W. GULL, Bart., and Portrait engraved on Steel by C. H. Jeens. Fourth Edition. Crown 8vo, 8s. 6d.

The Mystery of Pain. New Edition. Fcap. 8vo, 1s.

HOLTHAM, E. G.—Eight Years in Japan, 1873-1881. Work, Travel, and Recreation. With three maps. Large crown 8vo, 9s.

HOOPER, Mary.—Little Dinners: How to Serve them with Elegance and Economy. Seventeenth Edition. Crown 8vo, 2s. 6d.

Cookery for Invalids, Persons of Delicate Digestion, and Children. Third Edition. Crown 8vo, 2s. 6d.

Every-Day Meals. Being Economical and Wholesome Recipes for Breakfast, Luncheon, and Supper. Fifth Edition, Crown 8vo, 2s. 6d.

HOPKINS, Ellice.—Life and Letters of James Hinton, with an Introduction by Sir W. W. GULL, Bart., and Portrait engraved on Steel by C. H. Jeens. Fourth Edition. Crown 8vo, 8s. 6d.

Work amongst Working Men. Fourth edition. Crown 8vo, 3s. 6d.

HOSPITALIER, E.—The Modern Applications of Electricity. Translated and Enlarged by JULIUS MAIER, Ph.D. 2 vols. With numerous Illustrations. Demy 8vo, 12s. 6d. each volume.
   VOL. I.—Electric Generators, Electric Light.
   VOL. II.—Telephone: Various Applications; Electrical Transmission of Energy.

Household Readings on Prophecy. By a Layman. Small crown 8vo, 3s. 6d.

HUGHES, Henry.—The Redemption of the World. Crown 8vo, 3s. 6d.

HUNTINGFORD, Rev. E., D.C.L.—The Apocalypse. With a Commentary and Introductory Essay. Demy 8vo, 9s.

HUTTON, Arthur, M.A.—The Anglican Ministry: Its Nature and Value in relation to the Catholic Priesthood. With a Preface by His Eminence CARDINAL NEWMAN. Demy 8vo, 14s.

HUTTON, Rev. C. F.—Unconscious Testimony; or, the Silent Witness of the Hebrew to the Truth of the Historical Scriptures. Crown 8vo, 2s. 6d.

IM THURN, Everard F.—Among the Indians of British Guiana. Being Sketches, chiefly anthropologic, from the Interior of British Guiana. With numerous Illustrations. Demy 8vo.

JENKINS, E., and RAYMOND, J.—**The Architect's Legal Handbook.** Third Edition, Revised. Crown 8vo, 6s.

JENKINS, Rev. R. C., M.A.—**The Privilege of Peter**, and the Claims of the Roman Church confronted with the Scriptures, the Councils, and the Testimony of the Popes themselves. Fcap. 8vo, 3s. 6d.

JERVIS, Rev. W. Henley.—**The Gallican Church and the Revolution.** A Sequel to the History of the Church of France, from the Concordat of Bologna to the Revolution. Demy 8vo, 18s.

JOEL, L.—**A Consul's Manual and Shipowner's and Shipmaster's Practical Guide in their Transactions Abroad.** With Definitions of Nautical, Mercantile, and Legal Terms; a Glossary of Mercantile Terms in English, French, German, Italian, and Spanish; Tables of the Money, Weights, and Measures of the Principal Commercial Nations and their Equivalents in British Standards; and Forms of Consular and Notarial Acts. Demy 8vo, 12s.

JOHNSTONE, C. F., M.A.—**Historical Abstracts:** being Outlines of the History of some of the less known States of Europe. Crown 8vo, 7s. 6d.

JOLLY, William, F.R.S.E., etc.—**The Life of John Duncan, Scotch Weaver and Botanist.** With Sketches of his Friends and Notices of his Times. Second Edition. Large crown 8vo, with etched portrait, 9s.

JONES, C. A.—**The Foreign Freaks of Five Friends.** With 30 Illustrations. Crown 8vo, 6s.

JOYCE, P. W., LL.D., etc.—**Old Celtic Romances.** Translated from the Gaelic. Crown 8vo, 7s. 6d.

JOYNES, J. L.—**The Adventures of a Tourist in Ireland.** Second edition. Small crown 8vo, 2s. 6d.

KAUFMANN, Rev. M., B.A.—**Socialism:** its Nature, its Dangers, and its Remedies considered. Crown 8vo, 7s. 6d.

Utopias; or, Schemes of Social Improvement, from Sir Thomas More to Karl Marx. Crown 8vo, 5s.

KAY, Joseph.—**Free Trade in Land.** Edited by his Widow. With Preface by the Right Hon. JOHN BRIGHT, M.P. Sixth Edition. Crown 8vo, 5s.

KEMPIS, Thomas à.—**Of the Imitation of Christ.** Parchment Library Edition, 6s.; or vellum, 7s. 6d. The Red Line Edition, fcap. 8vo, red edges, 2s. 6d. The Cabinet Edition, small 8vo, cloth limp, 1s.; cloth boards, red edges, 1s. 6d. The Miniature Edition, red edges, 32mo, 1s.

** All the above Editions may be had in various extra bindings.

KENT, C.—**Corona Catholica ad Petri successoris Pedes Oblata; De Summi Pontificis Leonis XIII. Assumptione Epigramma.** In Quinquaginta Linguis. Fcap. 4to, 15s.

KETTLEWELL, Rev. S.—**Thomas à Kempis and the Brothers of Common Life.** 2 vols. With Frontispieces. Demy 8vo, 30s.

KIDD, Joseph, M.D.—**The Laws of Therapeutics**; or, the Science and Art of Medicine. Second Edition. Crown 8vo, 6s.

KINGSFORD, Anna, M.D.—**The Perfect Way in Diet.** A Treatise advocating a Return to the Natural and Ancient Food of our Race. Small crown 8vo, 2s.

KINGSLEY, Charles, M.A.—**Letters and Memories of his Life.** Edited by his Wife. With two Steel Engraved Portraits, and Vignettes on Wood. Thirteenth Cabinet Edition. 2 vols. Crown 8vo, 12s.

*** Also a New and Condensed Edition, in one volume. With Portrait. Crown 8vo, 6s.

All Saints' Day, and other Sermons. Also a new and condensed Edition in one volume, with Portrait. Crown 8vo, 6s. Edited by the Rev. W. HARRISON. Third Edition. Crown 8vo, 7s. 6d.

True Words for Brave Men. A Book for Soldiers' and Sailors' Libraries. Tenth Edition. Crown 8vo, 2s. 6d.

KNOX, Alexander A.—**The New Playground**; or, Wanderings in Algeria. New and cheaper edition. Large crown 8vo, 6s.

LANDON Joseph.—**School Management**; Including a General View of the Work of Education, Organization, and Discipline. Second Edition. Crown 8vo, 6s.

LAURIE, S. S.—**The Training of Teachers,** and other Educational Papers. Crown 8vo, 7s. 6d.

LEE, Rev. F. G., D.C.L.—**The Other World**; or, Glimpses of the Supernatural. 2 vols. A New Edition. Crown 8vo, 15s.

Letters from a Young Emigrant in Manitoba. Second Edition. Small crown 8vo, 3s. 6d.

LEWIS, Edward Dillon.—**A Draft Code of Criminal Law and Procedure.** Demy 8vo, 21s.

LILLIE, Arthur, M.R.A.S.—**The Popular Life of Buddha.** Containing an Answer to the Hibbert Lectures of 1881. With Illustrations. Crown 8vo, 6s.

LINDSAY, W. Lauder, M.D.—**Mind in the Lower Animals in Health and Disease.** 2 vols. Demy 8vo, 32s.

Vol. I.—Mind in Health. Vol. II.—Mind in Disease.

LLOYD, Walter.—**The Hope of the World:** An Essay on Universal Redemption. Crown 8vo, 5s.

LONSDALE, Margaret.—**Sister Dora:** a Biography. With Portrait. Twenty-fifth Edition. Crown 8vo, 2s. 6d.

LOWDER, Charles.—**A Biography.** By the Author of "St. Teresa." New and Cheaper Edition. Crown 8vo. With Portrait. 3s. 6d.

LYTTON, Edward Bulwer, Lord.—Life, Letters and Literary Remains. By his Son, The EARL OF LYTTON. With Portraits, Illustrations and Facsimiles. Demy 8vo.
[Vols. I. and II. just ready.

MACHIAVELLI, Niccolò.—Discourses on the First Decade of Titus Livius. Translated from the Italian by NINIAN HILL THOMSON, M.A. Large crown 8vo, 12s.

The Prince. Translated from the Italian by N. H. T. Small crown 8vo, printed on hand-made paper, bevelled boards, 6s.

MACKENZIE, Alexander.—How India is Governed. Being an Account of England's Work in India. Small crown 8vo, 2s.

MACNAUGHT, Rev. John.—Cœna Domini: An Essay on the Lord's Supper, its Primitive Institution, Apostolic Uses, and Subsequent History. Demy 8vo, 14s.

MACWALTER, Rev. G. S.—Life of Antonis Rosmini Serbati (Founder of the Institute of Charity). 2 vols. Demy 8vo.
[Vol. I. now ready, price 12s.

MAGNUS, Mrs.—About the Jews since Bible Times. From the Babylonian Exile till the English Exodus. Small crown 8vo, 6s.

MAIR, R. S., M.D., F.R.C.S.E.—The Medical Guide for Anglo-Indians. Being a Compendium of Advice to Europeans in India, relating to the Preservation and Regulation of Health. With a Supplement on the Management of Children in India. Second Edition. Crown 8vo, limp cloth, 3s. 6d.

MALDEN, Henry Elliot.—Vienna, 1683. The History and Consequences of the Defeat of the Turks before Vienna, September 12th, 1683, by John Sobieski, King of Poland, and Charles Leopold, Duke of Lorraine. Crown 8vo, 4s. 6d.

Many Voices. A volume of Extracts from the Religious Writers of Christendom from the First to the Sixteenth Century. With Biographical Sketches. Crown 8vo, cloth extra, red edges, 6s.

MARKHAM, Capt. Albert Hastings, R.N.—The Great Frozen Sea: A Personal Narrative of the Voyage of the *Alert* during the Arctic Expedition of 1875-6. With 6 Full-page Illustrations, 2 Maps, and 27 Woodcuts. Sixth and Cheaper Edition. Crown 8vo, 6s.

A Polar Reconnaissance: being the Voyage of the *Isbjörn* to Novaya Zemlya in 1879. With 10 Illustrations. Demy 8vo, 16s.

Marriage and Maternity; or, Scripture Wives and Mothers. Small crown 8vo, 4s. 6d.

MARTINEAU, Gertrude.—Outline Lessons on Morals. Small crown 8vo, 3s. 6d.

MAUDSLEY, H., M.D.—Body and Will. Being an Essay concerning Will, in its Metaphysical, Physiological, and Pathological Aspects. 8vo, 12s.

McGRATH, Terence.—Pictures from Ireland. New and Cheaper Edition. Crown 8vo, 2s.

MEREDITH, M.A.—Theotokos, the Example for Woman. Dedicated, by permission, to Lady Agnes Wood. Revised by the Venerable Archdeacon DENISON. 32mo, limp cloth, 1s. 6d.

MILLER, Edward.—The History and Doctrines of Irvingism; or, the so-called Catholic and Apostolic Church. 2 vols. Large post 8vo, 25s.

The Church in Relation to the State. Large crown 8vo, 7s. 6d.

MINCHIN, J. G.—Bulgaria since the War: Notes of a Tour in the Autumn of 1879. Small crown 8vo, 3s. 6d.

MITFORD, Bertram.—Through the Zulu Country. Its Battle-fields and its People. With five Illustrations. Demy 8vo, 14s.

MIVART, St. George.—Nature and Thought: An Introduction to a Natural Philosophy. Demy 8vo, 10s. 6d.

MOCKLER, E.—A Grammar of the Baloochee Language, as it is spoken in Makran (Ancient Gedrosia), in the Persia-Arabic and Roman characters. Fcap. 8vo, 5s.

MOLESWORTH, Rev. W. Nassau, M.A.—History of the Church of England from 1660. Large crown 8vo, 7s. 6d.

MORELL, J. R.—Euclid Simplified in Method and Language. Being a Manual of Geometry. Compiled from the most important French Works, approved by the University of Paris and the Minister of Public Instruction. Fcap. 8vo, 2s. 6d.

MORSE, E. S., Ph.D.—First Book of Zoology. With numerous Illustrations. New and Cheaper Edition. Crown 8vo, 2s. 6d.

MURPHY, John Nicholas.—The Chair of Peter; or, the Papacy considered in its Institution, Development, and Organization, and in the Benefits which for over Eighteen Centuries it has conferred on Mankind. Demy 8vo, 18s.

NELSON, J. H., M.A.—A Prospectus of the Scientific Study of the Hindû Law. Demy 8vo, 9s.

NEWMAN, J. H., D.D.—Characteristics from the Writings of. Being Selections from his various Works. Arranged with the Author's personal Approval. Sixth Edition. With Portrait. Crown 8vo, 6s.

** A Portrait of Cardinal Newman, mounted for framing, can be had, 2s. 6d.

NEWMAN, Francis William.—Essays on Diet. Small crown 8vo, cloth limp, 2s.

New Werther. By LOKI. Small crown 8vo, 2s. 6d.

NICHOLSON, Edward Byron.—**The Gospel according to the Hebrews.** Its Fragments Translated and Annotated with a Critical Analysis of the External and Internal Evidence relating to it. Demy 8vo, 9s. 6d.

A New Commentary on the Gospel according to Matthew. Demy 8vo, 12s.

NICOLS, Arthur, F.G.S., F.R.G.S.—**Chapters from the Physical History of the Earth:** an Introduction to Geology and Palæontology. With numerous Illustrations. Crown 8vo, 5s.

NOPS, Marianne.—**Class Lessons on Euclid.** Part I. containing the First two Books of the Elements. Crown 8vo, 2s. 6d.

Notes on St. Paul's Epistle to the Galatians. For Readers of the Authorized Version or the Original Greek. Demy 8vo, 2s. 6d.

Nuces: EXERCISES ON THE SYNTAX OF THE PUBLIC SCHOOL LATIN PRIMER. New Edition in Three Parts. Crown 8vo, each 1s.
*** The Three Parts can also be had bound together, 3s.

OATES, Frank, F.R.G.S.—**Matabele Land and the Victoria Falls.** A Naturalist's Wanderings in the Interior of South Africa. Edited by C. G. OATES, B.A. With numerous Illustrations and 4 Maps. Demy 8vo, 21s.

OGLE, W., M.D., F.R.C.P.—**Aristotle on the Parts of Animals.** Translated, with Introduction and Notes. Royal 8vo, 12s. 6d.

Oken Lorenz, Life of. By ALEXANDER ECKER. With Explanatory Notes, Selections from Oken's Correspondence, and Portrait of the Professor. From the German by ALFRED TULK. Crown 8vo, 6s.

O'MEARA, Kathleen.—**Frederic Ozanam,** Professor of the Sorbonne: His Life and Work. Second Edition. Crown 8vo, 7s. 6d.

Henri Perreyve and his Counsels to the Sick. Small crown 8vo, 5s..

OSBORNE, Rev. W. A.—**The Revised Version of the New Testament.** A Critical Commentary, with Notes upon the Text. Crown 8vo, 5s.

OTTLEY, H. Bickersteth.—**The Great Dilemma.** Christ His Own Witness or His Own Accuser. Six Lectures. Second Edition. Crown 8vo, 3s. 6d.

Our Public Schools—Eton, Harrow, Winchester, Rugby, Westminster, Marlborough, The Charterhouse. Crown 8vo, 6s.

OWEN, F. M.—**John Keats:** a Study. Crown 8vo, 6s.

OWEN, Rev. Robert, B.D.—**Sanctorale Catholicum;** or, Book of Saints. With Notes, Critical, Exegetical, and Historical. Demy 8vo, 18s.

OXENHAM, Rev. F. Nutcombe.—**What is the Truth as to Everlasting Punishment.** Part II. Being an Historical Inquiry into the Witness and Weight of certain Anti-Origenist Councils. Crown 8vo, 2s. 6d.

OXONIENSES.—**Romanism, Protestantism, Anglicanism.** Being a Layman's View of some questions of the Day. Together with Remarks on Dr. Littledale's "Plain Reasons against joining the Church of Rome." Crown 8vo, 3s. 6d.

PALMER, the late William.—**Notes of a Visit to Russia in 1840-1841.** Selected and arranged by JOHN H. CARDINAL NEWMAN, with portrait. Crown 8vo, 8s. 6d.

Parchment Library. Choicely Printed on hand-made paper, limp parchment antique, 6s.; vellum, 7s. 6d. each volume.

English Lyrics.

The Sonnets of John Milton. Edited by MARK PATTISON. With Portrait after Vertue.

Poems by Alfred Tennyson. 2 vols. With minature frontispieces by W. B. Richmond.

French Lyrics. Selected and Annotated by GEORGE SAINTSBURY. With a minature frontispiece designed and etched by H. G. Glindoni.

The Fables of Mr. John Gay. With Memoir by AUSTIN DOBSON, and an etched portrait from an unfinished Oil Sketch by Sir Godfrey Kneller.

Select Letters of Percy Bysshe Shelley. Edited, with an Introduction, by RICHARD GARNETT.

The Christian Year. Thoughts in Verse for the Sundays and Holy Days throughout the Year. With Miniature Portrait of the Rev. J. Keble, after a Drawing by G. Richmond, R.A.

Shakspere's Works. Complete in Twelve Volumes.

Eighteenth Century Essays. Selected and Edited by AUSTIN DOBSON. With a Miniature Frontispiece by R. Caldecott.

Q. Horati Flacci Opera. Edited by F. A. CORNISH, Assistant Master at Eton. With a Frontispiece after a design by L. Alma Tadema, etched by Leopold Lowenstam.

Edgar Allan Poe's Poems. With an Essay on his Poetry by ANDREW LANG, and a Frontispiece by Linley Sambourne.

Shakspere's Sonnets. Edited by EDWARD DOWDEN. With a Frontispiece etched by Leopold Lowenstam, after the Death Mask.

English Odes. Selected by EDMUND W. GOSSE. With Frontispiece on India paper by Hamo Thornycroft, A.R.A.

Of the Imitation of Christ. By THOMAS À KEMPIS. A revised Translation. With Frontispiece on India paper, from a Design by W. B. Richmond.

Parchment Library—*continued.*

Tennyson's The Princess: a Medley. With a Miniature Frontispiece by H. M. Paget, and a Tailpiece in Outline by Gordon Browne.

Poems: Selected from PERCY BYSSHE SHELLEY. Dedicated to Lady Shelley. With a Preface by RICHARD GARNETT and a Miniature Frontispiece.

Tennyson's "In Memoriam." With a Miniature Portrait in *eau-forte* by Le Rat, after a Photograph by the late Mrs. Cameron.

PARSLOE, Joseph.—**Our Railways.** Sketches, Historical and Descriptive. With Practical Information as to Fares and Rates, etc., and a Chapter on Railway Reform. Crown 8vo, 6s.

PAUL, C. Kegan.—Biographical Sketches. Printed on hand-made paper, bound in buckram. Second Edition. Crown 8vo, 7s. 6d.

PAUL, Alexander.—**Short Parliaments.** A History of the National Demand for frequent General Elections. Small crown 8vo, 3s. 6d.

PEARSON, Rev. S.—**Week-day Living.** A Book for Young Men and Women. Second Edition. Crown 8vo, 5s.

PENRICE, Maj. J., B.A.—**A Dictionary and Glossary of the Ko-ran.** With Copious Grammatical References and Explanations of the Text. 4to, 21s.

PESCHEL, Dr. Oscar.—**The Races of Man and their Geographical Distribution.** Large crown 8vo, 9s.

PETERS, F. H.—**The Nicomachean Ethics of Aristotle.** Translated by. Crown 8vo, 6s.

PHIPSON, E.—**The Animal Lore of Shakspeare's Time.** Including Quadrupeds, Birds, Reptiles, Fish and Insects. Large post 8vo, 9s.

PIDGEON, D.—**An Engineer's Holiday;** or, Notes of a Round Trip from Long. 0° to 0°. New and Cheaper Edition. Large crown 8vo, 7s. 6d.

PRICE, Prof. Bonamy.—**Currency and Banking.** Crown 8vo, 6s.

Chapters on Practical Political Economy. Being the Substance of Lectures delivered before the University of Oxford. New and Cheaper Edition. Large post 8vo, 5s.

Pulpit Commentary, The. (Old Testament Series.) Edited by the Rev. J. S. EXELL and the Rev. Canon H. D. M. SPENCE.

Genesis. By the Rev. T. WHITELAW, M.A.; with Homilies by the Very Rev. J. F. MONTGOMERY, D.D., Rev. Prof. R. A. REDFORD, M.A., LL.B., Rev. F. HASTINGS, Rev. W. ROBERTS, M.A. An Introduction to the Study of the Old Testament by the Venerable Archdeacon FARRAR, D.D., F.R.S.; and Introductions to the Pentateuch by the Right Rev. H. COTTERILL, D.D., and Rev. T. WHITELAW, M.A. Seventh Edition. 1 vol., 15s.

Pulpit Commentary, The—*continued.*

Exodus. By the Rev. Canon RAWLINSON. With Homilies by Rev. J. ORR, Rev. D. YOUNG, Rev. C. A. GOODHART, Rev. J. URQUHART, and the Rev. H. T. ROBJOHNS. Third Edition. 2 vols., 18s.

Leviticus. By the Rev. Prebendary MEYRICK, M.A. With Introductions by the Rev. R. COLLINS, Rev. Professor A. CAVE, and Homilies by Rev. Prof. REDFORD, LL.B., Rev. J. A. MACDONALD, Rev. W. CLARKSON, Rev. S. R. ALDRIDGE, LL.B., and Rev. MCCHEYNE EDGAR. Fourth Edition. 15s.

Numbers. By the Rev. R. WINTERBOTHAM, LL.B.; with Homilies by the Rev. Professor W. BINNIE, D.D., Rev. E. S. PROUT, M.A., Rev. D. YOUNG, Rev. J. WAITE, and an Introduction by the Rev. THOMAS WHITELAW, M.A. Fourth Edition. 15s.

Deuteronomy. By the Rev. W. L. ALEXANDER, D.D. With Homilies by Rev. C. CLEMANCE, D.D., Rev. J. ORR, B.D., Rev. R. M. EDGAR, M.A., Rev. D. DAVIES, M.A. Third edition. 15s.

Joshua. By Rev. J. J. LIAS, M.A.; with Homilies by Rev. S. R. ALDRIDGE, LL.B., Rev. R. GLOVER, REV. E. DE PRESSENSÉ, D.D., Rev. J. WAITE, B.A., Rev. F. W. ADENEY, M.A.; and an Introduction by the Rev. A. PLUMMER, M.A. Fifth Edition. 12s. 6d.

Judges and Ruth. By the Bishop of Bath and Wells, and Rev. J. MORRISON, D.D.; with Homilies by Rev. A. F. MUIR, M.A., Rev. W. F. ADENEY, M.A., Rev. W. M. STATHAM, and Rev. Professor J. THOMSON, M.A. Fourth Edition. 10s. 6d.

1 Samuel. By the Very Rev. R. P. SMITH, D.D.; with Homilies by Rev. DONALD FRASER, D.D., Rev. Prof. CHAPMAN, and Rev. B. DALE. Sixth Edition. 15s.

1 Kings. By the Rev. JOSEPH HAMMOND, LL.B. With Homilies by the Rev. E. DE PRESSENSÉ, D.D., Rev. J. WAITE, B.A., Rev. A. ROWLAND, LL.B., Rev. J. A. MACDONALD, and Rev. J. URQUHART. Fourth Edition. 15s.

Ezra, Nehemiah, and Esther. By Rev. Canon G. RAWLINSON, M.A.; with Homilies by Rev. Prof. J. R. THOMSON, M.A., Rev. Prof. R. A. REDFORD, LL.B., M.A., Rev. W. S. LEWIS, M.A., Rev. J. A. MACDONALD, Rev. A. MACKENNAL, B.A., Rev. W. CLARKSON, B.A., Rev. F. HASTINGS, Rev. W. DINWIDDIE, LL.B., Rev. Prof. ROWLANDS, B.A., Rev. G. WOOD, B.A., Rev. Prof. P. C. BARKER, LL.B., M.A., and the Rev. J. S. EXELL. Sixth Edition. 1 vol., 12s. 6d.

Jeremiah. By the Rev. J. K. CHEYNE, M.A.; with Homilies by the Rev. W. F. ADENEY, M.A., Rev. A. F. MUIR, M.A., Rev. S. CONWAY, B.A., Rev. J. WAITE, B.A., and Rev. D. YOUNG, B.A. Vol. I., 15s.

Pulpit Commentary, The. (New Testament Series.) St. Mark. By Very Rev. E. BICKERSTETH, D.D., Dean of Lichfield; with Homilies by Rev. Prof. THOMSON, M.A., Rev. Prof. GIVEN, M.A., Rev. Prof. JOHNSON, M.A., Rev. A. ROWLAND, B.A., LL.B., Rev. A. MUIR, and Rev. R. GREEN. 2 vols. Third Edition. 21s.

PUSEY, Dr.—Sermons for the Church's Seasons from Advent to Trinity. Selected from the Published Sermons of the late EDWARD BOUVERIE PUSEY, D.D. Crown 8vo, 5s.

QUILTER, Harry.—"The Academy," 1872-1882.

RADCLIFFE, Frank R. Y.—The New Politicus. Small crown 8vo, 2s. 6d.

Realities of the Future Life. Small crown 8vo, 1s. 6d.

RENDELL, J. M.—Concise Handbook of the Island of Madeira. With Plan of Funchal and Map of the Island. Fcap. 8vo, 1s. 6d.

REYNOLDS, Rev. J. W.—The Supernatural in Nature. A Verification by Free Use of Science. Third Edition, Revised and Enlarged. Demy 8vo, 14s.

The Mystery of Miracles. Third and Enlarged Edition. Crown 8vo, 6s.

RIBOT, Prof. Th.—Heredity: A Psychological Study on its Phenomena, its Laws, its Causes, and its Consequences. Large crown 8vo, 9s.

ROBERTSON, The late Rev. F. W., M.A.—Life and Letters of. Edited by the Rev. STOPFORD BROOKE, M.A.
    I. Two vols., uniform with the Sermons. With Steel Portrait. Crown 8vo, 7s. 6d.
    II. Library Edition, in Demy 8vo, with Portrait. 12s.
    III. A Popular Edition, in 1 vol. Crown 8vo, 6s.

Sermons. Four Series. Small crown 8vo, 3s. 6d. each.

The Human Race, and other Sermons. Preached at Cheltenham, Oxford, and Brighton. New and Cheaper Edition. Crown 8vo, 3s. 6d.

Notes on Genesis. New and Cheaper Edition. Crown 8vo, 3s. 6d.

Expository Lectures on St. Paul's Epistles to the Corinthians. A New Edition. Small crown 8vo, 5s.

Lectures and Addresses, with other Literary Remains. A New Edition. Crown 8vo, 5s.

An Analysis of Mr. Tennyson's "In Memoriam." (Dedicated by Permission to the Poet-Laureate.) Fcap. 8vo, 2s.

The Education of the Human Race. Translated from the German of GOTTHOLD EPHRAIM LESSING. Fcap. 8vo, 2s. 6d.

The above Works can also be had, bound in half morocco.

⁎⁎ A Portrait of the late Rev. F. W. Robertson, mounted for framing, can be had, 2s. 6d.

Rosmini Serbati (Life of). By G. STUART MACWALTER. 2 vols. 8vo. [Vol. I. now ready, 12s.

Rosmini's Origin of Ideas. Translated from the Fifth Italian Edition of the Nuovo Saggio *Sull' origine delle idee.* 3 vols. Demy 8vo, cloth. [Vols. I. and II. now ready, 16s. each.

Rosmini's Philosophical System. Translated, with a Sketch of the Author's Life, Bibliography, Introduction, and Notes by THOMAS DAVIDSON. Demy 8vo, 16s.

RULE, Martin, M.A.—**The Life and Times of St. Anselm, Archbishop of Canterbury and Primate of the Britains.** 2 vols. Demy 8vo, 21s.

SALVATOR, Archduke Ludwig.—Levkosia, the Capital of Cyprus. Crown 4to, 10s. 6d.

SAMUEL, Sydney M.—Jewish Life in the East. Small crown 8vo, 3s. 6d.

SAYCE, Rev. Archibald Henry.—Introduction to the Science of Language. 2 vols. Second Edition. Large post 8vo, 25s.

Scientific Layman. The New Truth and the Old Faith: are they Incompatible? Demy 8vo, 10s. 6d.

SCOONES, W. Baptiste.—**Four Centuries of English Letters:** A Selection of 350 Letters by 150 Writers, from the Period of the Paston Letters to the Present Time. Third Edition. Large crown 8vo, 6s.

SHILLITO, Rev. Joseph.—Womanhood: its Duties, Temptations, and Privileges. A Book for Young Women. Third Edition. Crown 8vo, 3s. 6d.

SHIPLEY, Rev. Orby, M.A.—**Principles of the Faith in Relation to Sin.** Topics for Thought in Times of Retreat. Eleven Addresses delivered during a Retreat of Three Days to Persons living in the World. Demy 8vo, 12s.

Sister Augustine, Superior of the Sisters of Charity at the St. Johannis Hospital at Bonn. Authorised Translation by HANS THARAU, from the German "Memorials of AMALIE VON LASAULX." Cheap Edition. Large crown 8vo, 4s. 6d.

SMITH, Edward, M.D., LL.B., F.R.S.—**Tubercular Consumption in its Early and Remediable Stages.** Second Edition. Crown 8vo, 6s.

SPEDDING, James.—**Reviews and Discussions, Literary, Political, and Historical not relating to Bacon.** Demy 8vo, 12s. 6d.

Evenings with a Reviewer; or, Bacon and Macaulay. With a Prefatory Notice by G. S. VENABLES, Q.C. 2 vols. Demy 8vo, 18s.

STAPFER, Paul.—Shakspeare and Classical Antiquity: Greek and Latin Antiquity as presented in Shakspeare's Plays. Translated by EMILY J. CAREY. Large post 8vo, 12s.

STEVENSON, Rev. W. F.—Hymns for the Church and Home. Selected and Edited by the Rev. W. FLEMING STEVENSON.
    The Hymn Book consists of Three Parts :—I. For Public Worship.—II. For Family and Private Worship.—III. For Children.
    ⁂ Published in various forms and prices, the latter ranging from 8d. to 6s.
    Lists and full particulars will be furnished on application to the Publishers.

STEVENSON, Robert Louis.—Travels with a Donkey in the Cevennes. With Frontispiece by Walter Crane. Small crown 8vo, 2s. 6d.

    An Inland Voyage. With Frontispiece by Walter Crane. Small Crown 8vo, 2s. 6d.

    Virginibus Puerisque, and other Papers. Crown 8vo, 6s.

Stray Papers on Education, and Scenes from School Life. By B. H. Small crown 8vo, 3s. 6d.

STRECKER-WISLICENUS.—Organic Chemistry. Translated and Edited, with Extensive Additions, by W. R. HODGKINSON, Ph.D., and A. J. GREENAWAY, F.I.C. Demy 8vo, 21s.

SULLY, James, M.A.—Pessimism : a History and a Criticism. Second Edition. Demy 8vo, 14s.

SWEDENBORG, Eman.—De Cultu et Amore Dei ubi Agitur de Telluris ortu, Paradiso et Vivario, tum de Primogeniti Seu Adami Nativitate Infantia, et Amore. Crown 8vo, 5s.

SYME, David.—Representative Government in England. Its Faults and Failures. Second Edition. Large crown 8vo, 6s.

TAYLOR, Rev. Isaac.—The Alphabet. An Account of the Origin and Development of Letters. With numerous Tables and Facsimiles. 2 vols. Demy 8vo, 36s.

Thirty Thousand Thoughts. Edited by the Rev. CANON SPENCE, Rev. J. S. EXELL, Rev. CHARLES NEIL, and Rev. JACOB STEPHENSON. 6 vols. Super royal 8vo.
    [Vol. I. now ready, 16s.

THOM, J. Hamilton.—Laws of Life after the Mind of Christ. Second Edition. Crown 8vo, 7s. 6d.

THOMSON, J. Turnbull.—Social Problems; or, An Inquiry into the Laws of Influence. With Diagrams. Demy 8vo, 10s. 6d.

TIDMAN, Paul F.—Gold and Silver Money. Part I.—A Plain Statement. Part II.—Objections Answered. Third Edition. Crown 8vo, 1s.

TIPPLE, Rev. S. A.—Sunday Mornings at Norwood. Prayers and Sermons. Crown 8vo, 6s.

TODHUNTER, Dr. J.—A Study of Shelley. Crown 8vo, 7s.

TREMENHEERE, Hugh Seymour, C.B.—A Manual of the Principles of Government, as set forth by the Authorities of Ancient and Modern Times. New and Enlarged Edition. Crown 8vo, 5s.

TUKE, Daniel Hack, M.D., F.R.C.P.—Chapters in the History of the Insane in the British Isles. With 4 Illustrations. Large crown 8vo, 12s.

TWINING, Louisa.—Workhouse Visiting and Management during Twenty-Five Years. Small crown 8vo, 3s. 6d.

TYLER, J.—The Mystery of Being: or, What Do We Know? Small crown 8vo, 3s. 6d.

UPTON, Major R. D.—Gleanings from the Desert of Arabia. Large post 8vo, 10s. 6d.

VACUUS, Viator.—Flying South. Recollections of France and its Littoral. Small crown 8vo, 3s. 6d.

VAUGHAN, H. Halford.—New Readings and Renderings of Shakespeare's Tragedies. 2 vols. Demy 8vo, 25s.

VILLARI, Professor.—Niccolò Machiavelli and his Times. Translated by Linda Villari. 4 vols. Large post 8vo, 48s.

VILLIERS, The Right Hon. C. P.—Free Trade Speeches of. With Political Memoir. Edited by a Member of the Cobden Club. 2 vols. With Portrait. Demy 8vo, 25s.

VOGT, Lieut.-Col. Hermann.—The Egyptian War of 1882. A translation. With Map and Plans. Large crown 8vo, 6s.

VOLCKXSOM, E. W. V.—Catechism of Elementary Modern Chemistry. Small crown 8vo, 3s.

VYNER, Lady Mary.—Every Day a Portion. Adapted from the Bible and the Prayer Book, for the Private Devotion of those living in Widowhood. Collected and Edited by Lady Mary Vyner. Square crown 8vo, 5s.

WALDSTEIN, Charles, Ph.D.—The Balance of Emotion and Intellect; an Introductory Essay to the Study of Philosophy. Crown 8vo, 6s.

WALLER, Rev. C. B.—The Apocalypse, reviewed under the Light of the Doctrine of the Unfolding Ages, and the Restitution of All Things. Demy 8vo, 12s.

WALPOLE, *Chas. George.*—History of Ireland from the Earliest Times to the Union with Great Britain. With 5 Maps and Appendices. Crown 8vo, 10s. 6d.

WALSHE, *Walter Hayle, M.D.*—Dramatic Singing Physiologically Estimated. Crown 8vo, 3s. 6d.

WEDMORE, *Frederick.*—The Masters of Genre Painting. With Sixteen Illustrations. Crown 8vo, 7s. 6d.

WHEWELL, *William, D.D.*—His Life and Selections from his Correspondence. By Mrs. STAIR DOUGLAS. With a Portrait from a Painting by Samuel Laurence. Demy 8vo, 21s.

WHITNEY, *Prof. William Dwight.*—Essentials of English Grammar, for the Use of Schools. Crown 8vo, 3s. 6d.

WILLIAMS, *Rowland, D.D.*—Psalms, Litanies, Counsels, and Collects for Devout Persons. Edited by his Widow. New and Popular Edition. Crown 8vo, 3s. 6d.

Stray Thoughts Collected from the Writings of the late Rowland Williams, D.D. Edited by his Widow. Crown 8vo, 3s. 6d.

WILLIS, *R., M.A.*—William Harvey. A History of the Discovery of the Circulation of the Blood: with a Portrait of Harvey after Faithorne. Demy 8vo, 14s.

WILSON, *Sir Erasmus.*—Egypt of the Past. With Chromo-lithograph and numerous Illustrations in the text. Second Edition, Revised. Crown 8vo, 12s.

The Recent Archaic Discovery of Egyptian Mummies at Thebes. A Lecture. Crown 8vo, 1s. 6d.

WILSON, *Lieut.-Col. C. T.*—The Duke of Berwick, Marshall of France, 1702-1734. Demy 8vo, 15s.

WOLTMANN, *Dr. Alfred, and* WOERMANN, *Dr. Karl.*—History of Painting. Edited by SIDNEY COLVIN. Vol. I. Painting in Antiquity and the Middle Ages. With numerous Illustrations. Medium 8vo, 28s.; bevelled boards, gilt leaves, 30s.

Word was Made Flesh. Short Family Readings on the Epistles for each Sunday of the Christian Year. Demy 8vo, 10s. 6d.

WREN, *Sir Christopher.*—His Family and His Times. With Original Letters, and a Discourse on Architecture hitherto unpublished. By LUCY PHILLIMORE. With Portrait. Demy 8vo, 14s.

YOUMANS, *Eliza A.*—First Book of Botany. Designed to Cultivate the Observing Powers of Children. With 300 Engravings. New and Cheaper Edition. Crown 8vo, 2s. 6d.

YOUMANS, *Edward L., M.D.*—A Class Book of Chemistry, on the Basis of the New System. With 200 Illustrations. Crown 8vo, 5s.

THE INTERNATIONAL SCIENTIFIC SERIES.

I. **Forms of Water:** a Familiar Exposition of the Origin and Phenomena of Glaciers. By J. Tyndall, LL.D., F.R.S. With 25 Illustrations. Eighth Edition. Crown 8vo, 5s.

II. **Physics and Politics;** or, Thoughts on the Application of the Principles of "Natural Selection" and "Inheritance" to Political Society. By Walter Bagehot. Sixth Edition. Crown 8vo, 4s.

III. **Foods.** By Edward Smith, M.D., LL.B., F.R.S. With numerous Illustrations. Eighth Edition. Crown 8vo, 5s.

IV. **Mind and Body:** the Theories of their Relation. By Alexander Bain, LL.D. With Four Illustrations. Seventh Edition. Crown 8vo, 4s.

V. **The Study of Sociology.** By Herbert Spencer. Eleventh Edition. Crown 8vo, 5s.

VI. **On the Conservation of Energy.** By Balfour Stewart, M.A., LL.D., F.R.S. With 14 Illustrations. Sixth Edition. Crown 8vo, 5s.

VII. **Animal Locomotion;** or Walking, Swimming, and Flying. By J. B. Pettigrew, M.D., F.R.S., etc. With 130 Illustrations. Third Edition. Crown 8vo, 5s.

VIII. **Responsibility in Mental Disease.** By Henry Maudsley, M.D. Fourth Edition. Crown 8vo, 5s.

IX. **The New Chemistry.** By Professor J. P. Cooke. With 31 Illustrations. Seventh Edition. Crown 8vo, 5s.

X. **The Science of Law.** By Professor Sheldon Amos. Fifth Edition. Crown 8vo, 5s.

XI. **Animal Mechanism:** a Treatise on Terrestrial and Aerial Locomotion. By Professor E. J. Marey. With 117 Illustrations. Third Edition. Crown 8vo, 5s.

XII. **The Doctrine of Descent and Darwinism.** By Professor Oscar Schmidt. With 26 Illustrations. Fifth Edition. Crown 8vo, 5s.

XIII. **The History of the Conflict between Religion and Science.** By J. W. Draper, M.D., LL.D. Seventeenth Edition. Crown 8vo, 5s.

XIV. **Fungi:** their Nature, Influences, Uses, etc. By M. C. Cooke, M.D., LL.D. Edited by the Rev. M. J. Berkeley, M.A., F.L.S. With numerous Illustrations. Third Edition. Crown 8vo, 5s.

XV. **The Chemical Effects of Light and Photography.** By Dr. Hermann Vogel. Translation thoroughly Revised. With 100 Illustrations. Fourth Edition. Crown 8vo, 5s.

XVI. **The Life and Growth of Language.** By Professor William Dwight Whitney. Fourth Edition. Crown 8vo, 5s.

XVII. **Money and the Mechanism of Exchange.** By W. Stanley Jevons, M.A., F.R.S. Sixth Edition. Crown 8vo, 5s.

XVIII. **The Nature of Light.** With a General Account of Physical Optics. By Dr. Eugene Lommel. With 188 Illustrations and a Table of Spectra in Chromo-lithography. Third Edition. Crown 8vo, 5s.

XIX. **Animal Parasites and Messmates.** By Monsieur Van Beneden. With 83 Illustrations. Third Edition. Crown 8vo, 5s.

XX. **Fermentation.** By Professor Schützenberger. With 28 Illustrations. Third Edition. Crown 8vo, 5s.

XXI. **The Five Senses of Man.** By Professor Bernstein. With 91 Illustrations. Fourth Edition. Crown 8vo, 5s.

XXII. **The Theory of Sound in its Relation to Music.** By Professor Pietro Blaserna. With numerous Illustrations. Third Edition. Crown 8vo, 5s.

XXIII. **Studies in Spectrum Analysis.** By J. Norman Lockyer, F.R.S. With six photographic Illustrations of Spectra, and numerous engravings on Wood. Third Edition. Crown 8vo, 6s. 6d.

XXIV. **A History of the Growth of the Steam Engine.** By Professor R. H. Thurston. With numerous Illustrations. Third Edition. Crown 8vo, 6s. 6d.

XXV. **Education as a Science.** By Alexander Bain, LL.D. Fourth Edition. Crown 8vo, 5s.

XXVI. **The Human Species.** By Professor A. de Quatrefages. Third Edition. Crown 8vo, 5s.

XXVII. **Modern Chromatics.** With Applications to Art and Industry. By Ogden N. Rood. With 130 original Illustrations. Second Edition. Crown 8vo, 5s.

XXVIII. **The Crayfish:** an Introduction to the Study of Zoology. By Professor T. H. Huxley. With 82 Illustrations. Third Edition. Crown 8vo, 5s.

XXIX. **The Brain as an Organ of Mind.** By H. Charlton Bastian, M.D. With numerous Illustrations. Third Edition. Crown 8vo, 5s.

XXX. **The Atomic Theory.** By Prof. Wurtz. Translated by G. Cleminshaw, F.C.S. Third Edition. Crown 8vo, 5s.

XXXI. **The Natural Conditions of Existence as they affect Animal Life.** By Karl Semper. With 2 Maps and 106 Woodcuts. Third Edition. Crown 8vo, 5s.

XXXII. **General Physiology of Muscles and Nerves.** By Prof. J. Rosenthal. Third Edition. With Illustrations. Crown 8vo, 5s.

XXXIII. **Sight:** an Exposition of the Principles of Monocular and Binocular Vision. By Joseph le Conte, LL.D. Second Edition. With 132 Illustrations. Crown 8vo, 5s.

XXXIV. **Illusions:** a Psychological Study. By James Sully. Second Edition. Crown 8vo, 5s.

XXXV. **Volcanoes: what they are and what they teach.** By Professor J. W. Judd, F.R.S. With 92 Illustrations on Wood. Second Edition. Crown 8vo, 5s.

XXXVI. **Suicide:** an Essay in Comparative Moral Statistics. By Prof. E. Morselli. Second Edition. With Diagrams. Crown 8vo, 5s.

XXXVII. **The Brain and its Functions.** By J. Luys. With Illustrations. Second Edition. Crown 8vo, 5s.

XXXVIII. **Myth and Science:** an Essay. By Tito Vignoli. Crown 8vo, 5s.

XXXIX. **The Sun.** By Professor Young. With Illustrations. Second Edition. Crown 8vo, 5s.

XL. **Ants, Bees, and Wasps:** a Record of Observations on the Habits of the Social Hymenoptera. By Sir John Lubbock, Bart., M.P. With 5 Chromo-lithographic Illustrations. Sixth Edition. Crown 8vo, 5s.

XLI. **Animal Intelligence.** By G. J. Romanes, LL.D., F.R.S. Third Edition. Crown 8vo, 5s.

XLII. **The Concepts and Theories of Modern Physics.** By J. B. Stallo. Second Edition. Crown 8vo, 5s.

XLIII. **Diseases of the Memory;** An Essay in the Positive Psychology. By Prof. Th. Ribot. Second Edition. Crown 8vo, 5s.

XLIV. **Man before Metals.** By N. Joly, with 148 Illustrations. Third Edition. Crown 8vo, 5s.

XLV. **The Science of Politics.** By Prof. Sheldon Amos. Second Edition. Crown 8vo, 5s.

XLVI. **Elementary Meteorology.** By Robert H. Scott. Second Edition. With Numerous Illustrations. Crown 8vo, 5s.

XLVII. **The Organs of Speech and their Application in the Formation of Articulate Sounds.** By George Hermann Von Meyer. With 47 Woodcuts. Crown 8vo, 5s.

XLVIII. **Fallacies.** A View of Logic from the Practical Side. By Alfred Sidgwick.

MILITARY WORKS.

BARRINGTON, Capt. J. T.—**England on the Defensive**; or, the Problem of Invasion Critically Examined. Large crown 8vo, with Map, 7s. 6d.

BRACKENBURY, Col. C. B., R.A., C.B.—**Military Handbooks for Regimental Officers.**

   I. **Military Sketching and Reconnaissance.** By Col. F. J. Hutchison, and Major H. G. MacGregor. Fourth Edition. With 15 Plates. Small 8vo, 6s.

   II. **The Elements of Modern Tactics Practically applied to English Formations.** By Lieut.-Col. Wilkinson Shaw. Fourth Edition. With 25 Plates and Maps. Small crown 8vo, 9s.

   III. **Field Artillery.** Its Equipment, Organization and Tactics. By Major Sisson C. Pratt, R.A. With 12 Plates. Second Edition. Small crown 8vo, 6s.

   IV. **The Elements of Military Administration.** First Part: Permanent System of Administration. By Major J. W. Buxton. Small crown 8vo. 7s. 6d.

   V. **Military Law**: Its Procedure and Practice. By Major Sisson C. Pratt, R.A. Small crown 8vo.

BROOKE, Major, C. K.—**A System of Field Training.** Small crown 8vo, cloth limp, 2s.

CLERY, C., Lieut.-Col.—**Minor Tactics.** With 26 Maps and Plans. Sixth and Cheaper Edition, Revised. Crown 8vo, 9s.

COLVILE, Lieut.-Col. C. F.—**Military Tribunals.** Sewed, 2s. 6d.

HARRISON, Lieut.-Col. R.—**The Officer's Memorandum Book for Peace and War.** Third Edition. Oblong 32mo, roan, with pencil, 3s. 6d.

Notes on Cavalry Tactics, Organisation, etc. By a Cavalry Officer. With Diagrams.. Demy 8vo, 12s.

PARR, Capt. H. Hallam, C.M.G.—**The Dress, Horses, and Equipment of Infantry and Staff Officers.** Crown 8vo, 1s.

SCHAW, Col. H.—**The Defence and Attack of Positions and Localities.** Second Edition, Revised and Corrected. Crown 8vo, 3s. 6d.

SHADWELL, Maj.-Gen., C.B.—**Mountain Warfare.** Illustrated by the Campaign of 1799 in Switzerland. Being a Translation of the Swiss Narrative compiled from the Works of the Archduke Charles, Jomini, and others. Also of Notes by General H. Dufour on the Campaign of the Valtelline in 1635. With Appendix, Maps, and Introductory Remarks. Demy 8vo, 16s.

STUBBS, *Lieut.-Col. F. W.*—The Regiment of Bengal Artillery. The History of its Organisation, Equipment, and War Services. Compiled from Published Works, Official Records, and various Private Sources. With numerous Maps and Illustrations. 2 vols. Demy 8vo, 32s.

POETRY.

ADAM OF ST. VICTOR.—The Liturgical Poetry of Adam of St. Victor. From the text of GAUTIER. With Translations into English in the Original Metres, and Short Explanatory Notes, by DIGBY S. WRANGHAM, M.A. 3 vols. Crown 8vo, printed on hand-made paper, boards, 21s.

AUCHMUTY, A. C.—Poems of English Heroism: From Brunanburh to Lucknow; from Athelstan to Albert. Small crown 8vo, 1s. 6d.

AVIA.—The Odyssey of Homer. Done into English Verse by. Fcap. 4to, 15s.

BANKS, Mrs. G. L.—Ripples and Breakers: Poems. Square 8vo, 5s.

BARNES, William.—Poems of Rural Life, in the Dorset Dialect. New Edition, complete in one vol. Crown 8vo, 8s. 6d.

BAYNES, Rev. Canon H. R.—Home Songs for Quiet Hours. Fourth and Cheaper Edition. Fcap. 8vo, cloth, 2s. 6d.
 ₊˟ This may also be had handsomely bound in morocco with gilt edges.

BENNETT, C. Fletcher.—Life Thoughts. A New Volume of Poems. With Frontispiece. Small crown 8vo.

BEVINGTON, L. S.—Key Notes. Small crown 8vo, 5s.

BILLSON, C. J.—The Acharnians of Aristophanes. Crown 8vo, 3s. 6d.

BOWEN, H. C., M.A.—Simple English Poems. English Literature for Junior Classes. In Four Parts. Parts I., II., and III., 6d. each, and Part IV., 1s.

BRYANT, W. C.—Poems. Red-line Edition. With 24 Illustrations and Portrait of the Author. Crown 8vo, extra, 7s. 6d.
 A Cheap Edition, with Frontispiece. Small crown 8vo, 3s. 6d.

BYRNNE, E. Fairfax.—Milicent: a Poem. Small crown 8vo, 6s.

Calderon's Dramas: the Wonder-Working Magician—Life is a Dream—the Purgatory of St. Patrick. Translated by DENIS FLORENCE MACCARTHY. Post 8vo, 10s.

Castilian Brothers (The), Chateaubriant, Waldemar: Three Tragedies; and **The Rose of Sicily:** a Drama. By the Author of "Ginevra," &c. Crown 8vo, 6s.

Chronicles of Christopher Columbus. A Poem in 12 Cantos. By M. D. C. Crown 8vo, 7s. 6d.

CLARKE, *Mary Cowden.*—**Honey from the Weed.** Verses. Crown 8vo, 7s.

COLOMB, *Colonel.*—**The Cardinal Archbishop:** a Spanish Legend. In 29 Cancions. Small crown 8vo, 5s.

CONWAY, *Hugh.*—**A Life's Idylls.** Small crown 8vo, 3s. 6d.

COPPÉE, *Francois.*—**L'Exilée.** Done into English Verse, with the sanction of the Author, by I. O. L. Crown 8vo, vellum, 5s.

COXHEAD, *Ethel.*—**Birds and Babies.** Imp. 16mo. With 33 Illustrations. Gilt, 2s. 6d.

David Rizzio, Bothwell, and the Witch Lady. Three Tragedies by the author of "Ginevra," etc. Crown 8vo, 6s.

DAVIE, *G. S., M.D.*—**The Garden of Fragrance.** Being a complete translation of the Bostán of Sádi from the original Persian into English Verse. Crown 8vo, 7s. 6d.

DAVIES, *T. Hart.*—**Catullus.** Translated into English Verse. Crown 8vo, 6s.

DE VERE, *Aubrey.*—**The Foray of Queen Meave,** and other Legends of Ireland's Heroic Age. Small crown 8vo, 5s.

Legends of the Saxon Saints. Small crown 8vo, 6s.

DILLON, *Arthur.*—**River Songs and other Poems.** With 13 autotype Illustrations from designs by Margery May. Fcap. 4to, cloth extra, gilt leaves, 10s. 6d.

DOBELL, *Mrs. Horace.*—**Ethelstone, Eveline,** and other Poems. Crown 8vo, 6s.

DOBSON, *Austin.*—**Old World Idylls** and other Poems. 18mo, cloth extra, gilt tops, 6s.

DOMET, *Alfred.*—**Ranolf and Amohia.** A Dream of Two Lives. New Edition, Revised. 2 vols. Crown 8vo, 12s.

Dorothy : a Country Story in Elegiac Verse. With Preface. Demy 8vo, 5s.

DOWDEN, *Edward, LL.D.*—**Shakspere's Sonnets.** With Introduction. Large post 8vo, 7s. 6d.

DOWNTON, *Rev. H., M.A.*—**Hymns and Verses.** Original and Translated. Small crown 8vo, 3s. 6d.

DUTT, *Toru.*—**A Sheaf Gleaned in French Fields.** New Edition. Demy 8vo, 10s. 6d.

EDMONDS, E. W.—Hesperas. Rhythm and Rhyme. Crown 8vo, 4s.

ELDRYTH, Maud.—Margaret, and other Poems. Small crown 8vo, 3s. 6d.

ELLIOTT, Ebenezer, The Corn Law Rhymer.—Poems. Edited by his son, the Rev. EDWIN ELLIOTT, of St. John's, Antigua. 2 vols. Crown 8vo, 18s.

English Odes. Selected, with a Critical Introduction by EDMUND W. GOSSE, and a miniature frontispiece by Hamo Thornycroft, A.R.A. Elzevir 8vo, limp parchment antique, 6s.; vellum, 7s. 6d.

EVANS, Anne.—Poems and Music. With Memorial Preface by ANN THACKERAY RITCHIE. Large crown 8vo, 7s.

GOSSE, Edmund W.—New Poems. Crown 8vo, 7s. 6d.

GRAHAM, William. Two Fancies and other Poems. Crown 8vo, 5s.

GRINDROD, Charles. Plays from English History. Crown 8vo, 7s. 6d.

GURNEY, Rev. Alfred.—The Vision of the Eucharist, and other Poems. Crown 8vo, 5s.

HELLON, H. G.—Daphnis: a Pastoral Poem. Small crown 8vo, 3s. 6d.

Herman Waldgrave: a Life's Drama. By the Author of "Ginevra," etc. Crown 8vo, 6s.

HICKEY, E. H.—A Sculptor, and other Poems. Small crown 8vo, 5s.

Horati Opera. Edited by F. A. CORNISH, Assistant Master at Eton. With a Frontispiece after a design by L. Alma Tadema, etched by Leopold Lowenstam. Parchment Library Edition, 6s.; vellum, 7s. 6d.

INGHAM, Sarson, C. J.—Cædmon's Vision, and other Poems. Small crown 8vo, 5s.

JENKINS, Rev. Canon.—Alfonso Petrucci, Cardinal and Conspirator: an Historical Tragedy in Five Acts. Small crown 8vo, 3s. 6d.

KING, Edward.—Echoes from the Orient. With Miscellaneous Poems. Small crown 8vo, 3s. 6d.

KING, Mrs. Hamilton.—The Disciples. Fifth Edition, with Portrait and Notes. Crown 8vo, 5s.

A Book of Dreams. Crown 8vo, 5s.

LANG, A.—XXXII Ballades in Blue China. Elzevir 8vo, parchment, 5s.

LAWSON, Right Hon. Mr. Justice.—**Hymni Usitati Latine Redditi** : with other Verses. Small 8vo, parchment, 5*s.*

LEIGH, Arran and Isla.—**Bellerophon.** Small crown 8vo, 5*s.*

LEIGHTON, Robert.—**Records,** and other Poems. With Portrait. Small crown 8vo, 7*s.* 6*d.*

Lessings Nathan the Wise. Translated by EUSTACE K. CORBETT. Crown 8vo, 6*s.*

Living English Poets MDCCCLXXXII. With Frontispiece by Walter Crane. Second Edition. Large crown 8vo. Printed on hand-made paper. Parchment, 12*s.*, vellum, 15*s.*

LOCKER, F.—**London Lyrics.** A New and Cheaper Edition. Small crown 8vo, 2*s.* 6*d.*

Love in Idleness. A Volume of Poems. With an etching by W. B. Scott. Small crown 8vo, 5*s.*

Love Sonnets of Proteus. With Frontispiece by the Author. Elzevir 8vo, 5*s.*

LOWNDES, Henry.—**Poems and Translations.** Crown 8vo, 6*s.*

LUMSDEN, Lieut.-Col. H. W.—**Beowulf** : an Old English Poem. Translated into Modern Rhymes. Second Edition. Small crown 8vo, 5*s.*

Lyre and Star. Poems by the Author of "Ginevra," etc. Crown 8vo, 5*s.*

MACLEAN, Charles Donald.—**Latin and Greek Verse Translations.** Small crown 8vo, 2*s.*

MAGNUSSON, Eirikr, M.A., and PALMER, E. H., M.A.—**Johan Ludvig Runeberg's Lyrical Songs, Idylls, and Epigrams.** Fcap. 8vo, 5*s.*

M.D.C.—**Chronicles of Christopher Columbus.** A Poem in Twelve Cantos. Crown 8vo, 7*s.* 6*d.*

MEREDITH, Owen, The Earl of Lytton.—**Lucile.** New Edition. With 32 Illustrations. 16mo, 3*s.* 6*d.* Cloth extra, gilt edges, 4*s.* 6*d.*

MIDDLETON, The Lady.—**Ballads.** Square 16mo, 3*s.* 6*d.*

MORICE, Rev. F. D., M.A.—**The Olympian and Pythian Odes of Pindar.** A New Translation in English Verse. Crown 8vo, 7*s.* 6*d.*

MORRIS, Lewis.—**Poetical Works of.** New and Cheaper Editions, with Portrait. Complete in 3 vols., 5*s.* each.

    Vol. I. contains "Songs of Two Worlds." Vol. II. contains "The Epic of Hades." Vol. III. contains "Gwen" and "The Ode of Life."

MORRIS, Lewis—continued.

The Epic of Hades. With 16 Autotype Illustrations, after the Drawings of the late George R. Chapman. 4to, cloth extra, gilt leaves, 25s.

The Epic of Hades. Presentation Edition. 4to, cloth extra, gilt leaves, 10s. 6d.

Ode of Life, The. Fourth Edition. Crown 8vo, 5s.

Songs Unsung. Fcap. 8vo.

MORSHEAD, E. D. A.—**The House of Atreus.** Being the Agamemnon, Libation-Bearers, and Furies of Æschylus. Translated into English Verse. Crown 8vo, 7s.

The Suppliant Maidens of Æschylus. Crown 8vo, 3s. 6d.

NADEN, Constance W.—**Songs and Sonnets of Spring Time.** Small crown 8vo, 5s.

NEWELL, E. J.—**The Sorrows of Simona and Lyrical Verses.** Small crown 8vo, 3s. 6d.

NOAKE, Major R. Compton.—**The Bivouac**; or, Martial Lyrist. With an Appendix: Advice to the Soldier. Fcap. 8vo, 5s. 6d.

NOEL, The Hon. Roden.—**A Little Child's Monument.** Second Edition. Small crown 8vo, 3s. 6d.

NORRIS, Rev. Alfred.—**The Inner and Outer Life.** Poems. Fcap. 8vo, 6s.

O'HAGAN, John.—**The Song of Roland.** Translated into English Verse. New and Cheaper Edition. Crown 8vo, 5s.

PFEIFFER, Emily.—**Glan Alarch: His Silence and Song: a Poem.** Second Edition. Crown 8vo, 6s.

Gerard's Monument, and other Poems. Second Edition. Crown 8vo, 6s.

Quarterman's Grace, and other Poems. Crown 8vo, 5s.

Poems. Second Edition. Crown 8vo, 6s.

Sonnets and Songs. New Edition. 16mo, handsomely printed and bound in cloth, gilt edges, 4s.

Under the Aspens; Lyrical and Dramatic. With Portrait. Crown 8vo, 6s.

PIKE, Warburton.—**The Inferno of Dante Allighieri.** Demy 8vo, 5s.

POE, Edgar Allan.—**Poems.** With an Essay on his Poetry by ANDREW LANG, and a Frontispiece by Linley Sambourne. Parchment Library Edition, 6s.; vellum, 7s. 6d.

Rare Poems of the 16th and 17th Centuries. Edited W. J. LINTON. Crown 8vo, 5*s*.

RHOADES, James.—**The Georgics of Virgil.** Translated into English Verse. Small crown 8vo, 5*s*.

ROBINSON, A. Mary F.—**A Handful of Honeysuckle.** Fcap. 8vo, 3*s*. 6*d*.

The Crowned Hippolytus. Translated from Euripides. With New Poems. Small crown 8vo, 5*s*.

SAUNDERS, John.—**Love's Martyrdom.** A Play and Poem. Small crown 8vo, 5*s*.

Schiller's Mary Stuart. German Text, with English Translation on opposite page by LEEDHAM WHITE. Crown 8vo, 6*s*.

SCOTT, George F. E.—**Theodora and other Poems.** Small 8vo, 3*s*. 6*d*.

SELKIRK, J. B.—**Poems.** Crown 8vo, 7*s*. 6*d*.

Shakspere's Sonnets. Edited by EDWARD DOWDEN. With a Frontispiece etched by Leopold Lowenstam, after the Death Mask. Parchment Library Edition, 6*s*. ; vellum, 7*s*. 6*d*.

Shakspere's Works. Complete in 12 Volumes. Parchment Library Edition, 6*s*. each ; vellum, 7*s*. 6*d*. each.

SHAW, W. F., M.A.—**Juvenal, Persius, Martial, and Catullus.** An Experiment in Translation. Crown 8vo, 5*s*.

SHELLEY, Percy Bysshe.—**Poems Selected from.** Dedicated to Lady Shelley. With Preface by RICHARD GARNETT. Parchment Library Edition, 6*s*. ; vellum, 7*s*. 6*d*.

Six Ballads about King Arthur. Crown 8vo, extra, gilt edges, 3*s*. 6*d*.

SLADEN, Douglas B.—**Frithjof and Ingebjorg, and other Poems.** Small crown 8vo, 5*s*.

TAYLOR, Sir H.—**Works.** Complete in Five Volumes. Crown 8vo, 30*s*.

Philip Van Artevelde. Fcap. 8vo, 3*s*. 6*d*.

The Virgin Widow, etc. Fcap. 8vo, 3*s*. 6*d*.

The Statesman. Fcap. 8vo, 3*s*. 6*d*.

TENNYSON, Alfred.—Works Complete :—

The Imperial Library Edition. Complete in 7 vols. Demy 8vo, 10*s*. 6*d*. each ; in Roxburgh binding, 12*s*. 6*d*. each.

Author's Edition. In 7 vols. Post 8vo, gilt 43*s*. 6*d*. ; or half-morocco, Roxburgh style, 54*s*.

Cabinet Edition. 13 vols. Each with Frontispiece. Fcap. 8vo, 2*s*. 6*d*. each.

Cabinet Edition. 13 vols. Complete in handsome Ornamental Case. 35*s*.

TENNYSON, Alfred—*continued.*

    The Royal Edition. In 1 vol. With 26 Illustrations and Portrait. Extra, bevelled boards, gilt leaves, 21s.

    The Guinea Edition. Complete in 13 vols. neatly bound and enclosed in box, 21s. ; French morocco or parchment, 31s. 6d.

    Shilling Edition. In 13 vols. pocket size, 1s. each, sewed.

    The Crown Edition. Complete in 1 vol. strongly bound, 6s. ; extra gilt leaves, 7s. 6d. ; Roxburgh, half-morocco, 8s. 6d.
        ⁎ Can also be had in a variety of other bindings.

    In Memoriam. With a Miniature Portrait in *eau-forte* by Le Rat, after a Photograph by the late Mrs. Cameron. Parchment Library Edition, 6s. ; vellum, 7s. 6d.

    The Princess. A Medley. With a Miniature Frontispiece by H. M. Paget, and a Tailpiece in Outline by Gordon Browne. Parchment Library Edition, 6s. ; vellum, 7s. 6d.

Original Editions :—

Poems. Small 8vo, 6s.

Maud, and other Poems. Small 8vo, 3s. 6d.

The Princess. Small 8vo, 3s. 6d.

Idylls of the King. Small 8vo, 5s.

Idylls of the King. Complete. Small 8vo, 6s.

The Holy Grail, and other Poems. Small 8vo, 4s. 6d.

Gareth and Lynette. Small 8vo, 3s.

Enoch Arden, etc. Small 8vo, 3s. 6d.

In Memoriam. Small 8vo, 4s.

Harold : a Drama. New Edition. Crown 8vo, 6s.

Queen Mary : a Drama. New Edition. Crown 8vo, 6s.

The Lover's Tale. Fcap. 8vo, 3s. 6d.

Ballads, and other Poems. Small 8vo, 5s.

Selections from the above Works. Super royal 16mo, 3s. 6d. ; gilt extra, 4s.

Songs from the above Works. 16mo, 2s. 6d.

  Tennyson for the Young and for Recitation. Specially arranged. Fcap. 8vo, 1s. 6d.

  The Tennyson Birthday Book. Edited by EMILY SHAKESPEAR. 32mo, limp, 2s. ; extra, 3s.
      ⁎ A superior Edition, printed in red and black, on antique paper, specially prepared. Small crown 8vo, extra, gilt leaves, 5s. ; and in various calf and morocco bindings.

THORNTON, L. M.—The Son of Shelomith. Small crown 8vo, 3s. 6d.

TODHUNTER, Dr. J.—Laurella, and other Poems. Crown 8vo, 6s. 6d.

    Forest Songs. Small crown 8vo, 3s. 6d.

    The True Tragedy of Rienzi: a Drama. 3s. 6d.

    Alcestis: a Dramatic Poem. Extra fcap. 8vo, 5s.

    A Study of Shelley. Crown 8vo, 7s.

    Translations from Dante, Petrarch, Michael Angelo, and Vittoria Colonna. Fcap. 8vo, 7s. 6d.

TURNER, Rev. C. Tennyson.—Sonnets, Lyrics, and Translations. Crown 8vo, 4s. 6d.

    Collected Sonnets, Old and New. With Prefatory Poem by ALFRED TENNYSON; also some Marginal Notes by S. T. COLERIDGE, and a Critical Essay by JAMES SPEDDING. Fcap. 8vo, 7s. 6d.

WALTERS, Sophia Lydia.—A Dreamer's Sketch Book. With 21 Illustrations by Percival Skelton, R. P. Leitch, W. H. J. Boot, and T. R. Pritchett. Engraved by J. D. Cooper. Fcap. 4to, 12s. 6d.

WEBSTER, Augusta.—In a Day: a Drama. Small crown 8vo, 2s. 6d.

Wet Days. By a Farmer. Small crown 8vo, 6s.

WILKINS, William.—Songs of Study. Crown 8vo, 6s.

WILLIAMS, J.—A Story of Three Years, and other Poems. Small crown 8vo, 3s. 6d.

YOUNGS, Ella Sharpe.—Paphus, and other Poems. Small crown 8vo, 3s. 6d.

WORKS OF FICTION IN ONE VOLUME.

BANKS, Mrs. G. L.—God's Providence House. New Edition. Crown 8vo, 3s. 6d.

HARDY, Thomas.—A Pair of Blue Eyes. Author of "Far from the Madding Crowd." New Edition. Crown 8vo, 6s.

    The Return of the Native. New Edition. With Frontispiece. Crown 8vo, 6s.

INGELOW, Jean.—Off the Skelligs: a Novel. With Frontispiece. Second Edition. Crown 8vo, 6s.

MACDONALD, G.—Castle Warlock. A Novel. New and Cheaper Edition. Crown 8vo, 6s.

MACDONALD, G.—continued.

    Malcolm. With Portrait of the Author engraved on Steel. Sixth Edition. Crown 8vo, 6s.

    The Marquis of Lossie. Fourth Edition. With Frontispiece. Crown 8vo, 6s.

    St. George and St. Michael. Third Edition. With Frontispiece. Crown 8vo, 6s.

PALGRAVE, W. Gifford.—**Hermann Agha**: an Eastern Narrative. Third Edition. Crown 8vo, 6s.

SHAW, Flora L.—**Castle Blair**; a Story of Youthful Lives. New and Cheaper Edition. Crown 8vo, 3s. 6d.

STRETTON, Hesba.—**Through a Needle's Eye**: a Story. New and Cheaper Edition, with Frontispiece. Crown 8vo, 6s.

TAYLOR, Col. Meadows, C.S.I., M.R.I.A.—**Seeta**: a Novel. New and Cheaper Edition. With Frontispiece. Crown 8vo, 6s.

    Tippoo Sultaun: a Tale of the Mysore War. New Edition, with Frontispiece. Crown 8vo, 6s.

    Ralph Darnell. New and Cheaper Edition. With Frontispiece. Crown 8vo, 6s.

    A Noble Queen. New and Cheaper Edition. With Frontispiece. Crown 8vo, 6s.

    The Confessions of a Thug. Crown 8vo, 6s.

    Tara: a Mahratta Tale. Crown 8vo, 6s.

Within Sound of the Sea. New and Cheaper Edition, with Frontispiece. Crown 8vo, 6s.

BOOKS FOR THE YOUNG.

Brave Men's Footsteps. A Book of Example and Anecdote for Young People. By the Editor of "Men who have Risen." With 4 Illustrations by C. Doyle. Eighth Edition. Crown 8vo, 3s. 6d.

COXHEAD, Ethel.—**Birds and Babies.** Imp. 16mo. With 33 Illustrations. Cloth gilt, 2s. 6d.

DAVIES, G. Christopher.—**Rambles and Adventures of our School Field Club.** With 4 Illustrations. New and Cheaper Edition. Crown 8vo, 3s. 6d.

EDMONDS, Herbert.—**Well Spent Lives**: a Series of Modern Biographies. New and Cheaper Edition. Crown 8vo, 3s. 6d.

EVANS, Mark.—**The Story of our Father's Love,** told to Children. Fourth and Cheaper Edition of Theology for Children. With 4 Illustrations. Fcap. 8vo, 1s. 6d.

JOHNSON, Virginia W.—**The Catskill Fairies.** Illustrated by Alfred Fredericks. 5s.

MAC KENNA, S. J.—**Plucky Fellows.** A Book for Boys. With 6 Illustrations. Fifth Edition. Crown 8vo, 3s. 6d.

REANEY, Mrs. G. S.—**Waking and Working;** or, From Girlhood to Womanhood. New and Cheaper Edition. With a Frontispiece. Crown 8vo, 3s. 6d.

> **Blessing and Blessed:** a Sketch of Girl Life. New and Cheaper Edition. Crown 8vo, 3s. 6d.
>
> **Rose Gurney's Discovery.** A Book for Girls. Dedicated to their Mothers. Crown 8vo, 3s. 6d.
>
> **English Girls:** Their Place and Power. With Preface by the Rev. R. W. Dale. Fourth Edition. Fcap. 8vo, 2s. 6d.
>
> **Just Anyone,** and other Stories. Three Illustrations. Royal 16mo, 1s. 6d.
>
> **Sunbeam Willie,** and other Stories. Three Illustrations. Royal 16mo, 1s. 6d.
>
> **Sunshine Jenny,** and other Stories. Three Illustrations. Royal 16mo, 1s. 6d.

STOCKTON, Frank R.—**A Jolly Fellowship.** With 20 Illustrations. Crown 8vo, 5s.

STORR, Francis, and TURNER, Hawes.—**Canterbury Chimes;** or, Chaucer Tales retold to Children. With 6 Illustrations from the Ellesmere MS. Second Edition. Fcap. 8vo, 3s. 6d.

STRETTON, Hesba.—**David Lloyd's Last Will.** With 4 Illustrations. New Edition. Royal 16mo, 2s. 6d.

Tales from Ariosto Re-told for Children. By a Lady. With 3 Illustrations. Crown 8vo, 4s. 6d.

WHITAKER, Florence.—**Christy's Inheritance.** A London Story. Illustrated. Royal 16mo, 1s. 6d.

PRINTED BY WILLIAM CLOWES AND SONS, LIMITED, LONDON AND BECCLES.

www.ingramcontent.com/pod-product-compliance
Lightning Source LLC
Chambersburg PA
CBHW031816230426
43669CB00009B/1162